THE JOYS OF
Christmas

A Glossary of Terms
and Traditions

Gisela A. Riedel Nolte

THE JOYS OF CHRISTMAS
Copyright © 2013 by Gisela A. Riedel Nolte

Cover photo credit: Harry Nolte
Arrangement by GARN

All rights reserved. Neither this publication nor any part of this publication may be reproduced or transmitted in any form or by any means, electronic or mechanical, including photocopying, recording or any information storage and retrieval system, without permission in writing from the author.

All Scripture quotations unless otherwise indicated are taken from the Revised Standard Version of the Bible, copyright 1952 [2nd edition, 1971] by the Division of Christian Education of the National Council of the Churches of Christ in the United States of America. Used by permission. All rights reserved.

Printed in Canada

ISBN: 978-1-77069-956-4

Word Alive Press
131 Cordite Road, Winnipeg, MB R3W 1S1
www.wordalivepress.ca

Library and Archives Canada Cataloguing in Publication

Nolte, Gisela A. Riedel, 1936, author
    The joys of Christmas / Gisela A. Riedel Nolte.

ISBN 978-1-77069-956-4 (pbk.)

    1. Christmas. I. Title.

GT4985.N65 2013   394.2663   C2013-902092-6

THIS BOOK IS DEDICATED TO THE GLORY AND HONOR OF THE

Author of Christmas

And to my parents:
Friedrich A. Riedel
Agathe M. Riedel, nee Tucholke
In grateful memory

Also with special affection to my children, grandchildren and my first great-grandson:
Harry and Denise Nolte,
Catherine and Andrew Nolte and baby Jackson,
Roy and Julie Nolte and Sara Nolte

Acknowledgements

Ever since I was a child, every year, when the Advent season approached, I was filled with a great excitement, almost, as if the real Christmas would happen again. This was due most likely to the teachings and preparations our parents made for us, and the glory of this event and celebration never waned in my life. As I grew older and I realized more fully that the human life consists not only of a physical and emotional, but also of a spiritual dimension, Christmas became ever more meaningful for me, but at the same time I was alarmed by the steady increase of secularization of the holidays. As I began to feel the urge to write a small book about Christmas, its meaning and traditions, joys and celebrations to help people understand the difference between the real Holy Days of the Season and the worldly festivities, friends, with whom I shared this plan immediately began to encourage me and willingly offered and provided their help in many ways. Also my family cheered me on and assisted on many levels. I am deeply thankful for all of their inspiration and assistance; without their indescribable kindness this book would not have been created. Instead of trying to mention some names and in the process forgetting others, I commit their names to the Golden Book in Heaven. I thank God for His blessings and inspirations and for all of you.

Foreword

Christmas is one of my favourite times of the year, as it is for so many. As the day approaches everywhere we look it seems there is some symbol of Christmas to remind us what this special day signifies. And yet for many these symbols have lost much of their meaning as we have lost our understanding of what they are meant to tell us. Gisela's book is a detailed guide to everything CHRISTMAS, from Angels to Zion and everything else in between. If you or your kids have ever wondered why we hang mistletoe, or what the angel Gabriel said to Mary you will find it in these pages. Whether you flip through the alphabetical list to find what you want or sit down and read it from cover to cover you will find lovingly written and joy-filled explanations of everything CHRISTMAS from an author who clearly loves her Lord and loves Christmas. And whatever you do, don't forget to try the cookie recipe on page 8!

God bless and Merry Christmas
The Reverend Blair Peever
Kingston, Ontario

Prologue

There is no holiday that is as beloved and celebrated as Christmas, together with the preceding Advent season to usher in this special festival, and it seems that not just in the Western world but all over the globe the joy and the fever of this holiday has, to some degree, infected people of every color, nationality, race and culture. Part of that is due to the great variety of goods that are manufactured far and near to supply the orders for gifts, decorative items and specialty foods, criss-crossing the globe to meet the demand. However, it does not come as a surprise to learn, that the real meaning of Christmas has become as colourful and camouflaged as combat outfits. Amidst the worldly hype of the season it is often hard to differentiate what is truth and what is fiction, and it seems that the fairytale aspect of it is ever increasing, overshadowing more and more this real and divine earth-shattering event: the birth of Jesus Christ, God's own Son, for our salvation.

There are, undoubtedly, many people who were raised with the full understanding of the reason for this observance. Parents, grandparents, family and friends, religious teachers, church school and catechism instructions have all contributed to the belief and the traditions with which this holiday is celebrated. Yet even among those who seemingly know what Christmas is all about, there are many questions for which the department stores, the flower shops and the bakeries have no answers. People flock to the churches on Christmas Eve or Christmas Day to worship and also out of tradition, and the sermons, the hymns and the prayers may be right on, but utter exhaustion or the anticipation simply block out some of what is heard and seen.

For many people the religious side of the holiday is unimportant; it is just that: a holiday – time off from work and school, an opportunity for family gatherings, good food, nice gifts, a change in activity and the monotony of life when the daylight is short and the weather is cold. It is easy to listen to and sing along with 'Frosty, The Snowman' or 'Jingle Bells', but the message of 'Joy To The World, The Lord has come' or 'Oh, Come All Ye Faithful' is no more than a familiar rhyme and melody and 'Silent Night' just a nice lullaby. But Christmas is so much more: God revealed His great love for us and sent His Son to live among us and to draw us back to the heart of the Father so that all of us believing in Him may live with Him forever. That is ultimately the desire of mankind, and this book wants to be a guide to that end. It is not a comprehensive work by any means but tries to give satisfying answers to many questions.

Scripture passages have been printed in *italics* for better recognition, and some words have been highlighted in **bold** for greater emphasis. The alphabetical order provides easy help in the search of subjects.

May the book be a blessing to all who look for the true meaning of Christmas and for those who wish to renew their faith and understanding of this wonderful event.

The Author

Contents

A — 1
ADVENT
ADVENT CALENDAR
ADVENT WREATH
ANGELS
ANIMALS
ANNA
AUGUSTUS

B — 7
BABY JESUS
BAKING and COOKING
BELLS
BETHLEHEM
BIBLE
BOXING DAY

C — 13
CANDLE MASS (see PURIFICATION)
CANDLES
CAROLS
CHRIST
CHRISTIANITY
CHRISTMAS
CHRISTMAS CAKE
CHURCH
CIRCUMCISION
CONCEPTION
CONTEMPLATION
CRAFTS
CRÈCHE

D — 22
DAVID
DECORATIONS
DOVE

E — 24
EGYPT
EPIPHANY

F — 25
FRANKINCENSE

G — 25
GENEALOGY
GIFTS
GLORY
GOLD

GOSPELS
GREETING CARDS
GUESTS

H 34
HEROD
HOLLY
HOLY

I 35
IMMACULATE CONCEPTION
INCARNATION
INN
INNOCENTS, HOLY (HOLY CHILDREN)
ISAIAH
ISRAEL

J 38
JERUSALEM
JESUS
JOHN THE BAPTIST
JOHN THE DISCIPLE
JOSEPH
JOY
JUDAISM

K 42
KINGS

L 42
LEVI
LIGHT
LUKE

M 43
MAGI (SEE WISE MEN)
MANGER
MARK

MARY, MOTHER OF JESUS
MARZIPAN
MATTHEW
MEDITATION
MESSIAH
MIDNIGHT MASS
MISTLETOE
MUSIC
MYRRH

N 48
NAZARETH
NEW YEAR
NUTS

O 49
ORNAMENTS

P 50
PEACE
PLUM PUDDING
POINSETTIA
PRAYER
PROPHETS
PUNCH
PURIFICATION (CANDLE MASS)
PYRAMIDS

Q 54
QUIRINIUS

R 54
RIBBONS

S 54
SANTA CLAUS
SAVIOR
SHEPHERDS
SIMEON

SNOW
SPICES
STABLE
STAR
ST. LUCIA
STOLLEN
STORY TELLING

T 60
TEMPLE
TINSEL
TREE
TRINITY
TWELVE DAYS OF CHRISTMAS

U 64
URGENCY/HASTE

V 65
VANILLA
VESPER
VESTMENTS
VIGIL
VIRGIN

W 66
WHITE
WISE MEN and MAGI
WREATHS

X 68
X-MAS

Y 68
YULE
YULE LOGS

Z 69
ZION

Epilogue 71

Bibliography 73

About the Author 77

The Joys of Christmas

ADVENT

It is very appropriate that a CHRISTMAS ALPHABET should begin with the word ADVENT. Advent means "to arrive". It describes the first coming of Christ, the Messiah, the Son of God, and is also applied to the Second Coming, called the Parousia, to establish His 1000 year reign.

The first Sunday in Advent signals the beginning of the Liturgical Year, i.e. the Church Year, in most Christian denominations.

The Church has designated the last four Sundays before Christmas – the 25th of December – to prepare the hearts of the believers, very similar to the weeks of Lent. The observances are called the "Four Sundays of Advent". They can begin as early as the 27th of November (the 4th, 11th, 18th of December) or as late as the 3rd of December (the 10th, 17th, 24th). The last Sunday of Advent can, therefore, fall on Christmas Eve, but never on Christmas Day.

Documents, when the Advent Season officially began, give conflicting information. In the year 524 A.D. at the Council of Lerida, a Spanish city in the Eastern Pyrenees, it was decided that weddings from the beginning of December until Christmas should be forbidden, so that joyful celebrations would not interfere with the observance of "quiet time" in preparation for the "Coming of the Lord". In Western Europe the Christmas cycle originally began on the day of St. Martin, the 11th of November because Christmas was celebrated on the 6th of January (the Baptism of the Lord), and forty days of fasting before Christmas were necessary. Since Saturdays and Sundays were excluded from fasting, the cycle had to begin on the 11th of November. This was later on changed. In Galicia in France the tradition of penitential preparation before Christmas began in the 6th century, and Pope Gregory the First (590-604) was instrumental for regulating the Advent liturgy.

The intention was to provide worshipers with time and opportunity to repent of their sins, to fast and pray. Preparations in the Orthodox Church for Christmas begin on the 15th of November. While some use the old Julian calendar with celebrations on January 7th, others have switched to December 25th of the Gregorian calendar.

The colors of the paraments, the ecclesiastical vestments and hangings in the church, reflect the liturgical season. During the weeks of Advent, purple, the same color as in Lent, was displayed because of the similarity of devotion and the penitent character, but was changed approximately four decades ago to blue. While the journey of Lent embraces the sorrow of Good Friday, the crucifixion and death of Christ, Advent anticipates the joy of Christmas, the Incarnation of God for the sake of man, hence the change in color to reflect this sentiment. But while Christmas colors explode in white, during Advent believers are still on the journey and have not yet arrived. New trends in interpretation and experience of worship rituals and liturgy demand flexibility.

Gert Lindner, in his book **Krippe und Stern (Manger and Star)** makes this observation that 'the Protestant Evangelical Churches to this day do not have a universal worship service for the weeks of Advent in preparation for Christmas'. (There may be some exceptions!) He quotes Hans Asmussen saying that in this regard the Roman Catholics are better equipped through regular prayer, song, the reading of scripture and the giving of alms to handle the demands of this trying season and to meet business people and taxed parents with more love and understanding. Amen to that!

ADVENT CALENDAR

Christmas is the most celebrated and anticipated holiday of the year and together with Easter the oldest of the Church year. Almost all people, even those who do not observe the religious aspect of it, whole-heartedly join in the festivities. It is especially a 'Season for the children', not only because of the expected gifts and the many lovely and colourful traditions, but also because it was initiated by a child, the Christ Child, the Son of God. Sadly, many people nowadays, children and adults alike, do not know the real meaning of Christmas anymore. To help children cope with the excitement and anticipation of three to four weeks of Advent before the **Big Day** and to help count the days until then, someone invented the Christmas calendar. It may be as old as the 19th century; some existing specimens date back to the early 20th century. They were made of four-sided cardboard in the shape of a house with a double layer of paper. The outside was artistically enhanced by seasonal motifs with closed windows that showed the dates from the 1st of Advent to the 24th of December. Every day one window would be opened and a printed scripture passage, usually a prophesy from the Old Testament would be revealed and read out loud for the whole family; sometimes a picture, relating to the Christmas event, could be seen. In the center of this paper house a candle would be placed to illuminate words and pictures. In those days many people, especially in rural areas, did not have electricity, and the use of candles was as common as the light bulb is today. The more windows were open, the brighter the contraption would shine, symbolizing the advancing light – Jesus Christ – that came into the world.

The counting of the days of Advent until Christmas may have had its origin in monastery schools where wooden boards were used to carve the dates into the wood. This tradition was well known in the alpine region of Central Europe. Until Advent calendars were commercially produced, the home-made versions took many shapes and forms, the most favourable was a wall hanging made with pockets, either of paper or material. Soon these pockets contained not only words and pictures, but also the occasional cookie or candy. Most markets, gift stores, book shops and grocery stores nowadays carry them: the outside colourful decorated with wintry, Christmassy, but predominantly non-religious scenes, and the pockets filled with a seasonally shaped piece of chocolate – sweet, yet another unfortunate development away from the true meaning of the season, i.e. fasting, prayer and contemplation.

ADVENT WREATH

Most Christian churches display a wreath of evergreens, usually made of fir, pine or spruce branches. The evergreen is a symbol of hope, the shape reflects the unending love of God and eternal life. The wreath holds four candles, three of which are blue, one is pink. On the first Sunday in Advent one blue candle is lit from a candle on the altar. On the second Sunday in Advent, two blue candles are lit; these first two candles and the readings center on the **Parousia**, the Second Coming of Christ. On the third Sunday in Advent all three blue candles are burning, and the focus is on **John the Baptist** as the herald of Jesus. On the fourth Sunday all four candles are lit; the pink candle is called the Angel's candle, signifying the visit of the angel Gabriel at the time of the annunciation to Mary. Some traditions place a white candle in the center of the wreath; it is the **Christ** candle and is lit on Christmas Eve. On Christmas Day the Advent candles remain unlit, only the Christ candle, the Baptismal candle and those on the altar are ignited.

Compared with the Christmas tree, which we will look at later, the wreath developed from an inspiration in the 19th century at *Das Rauhe Haus* (THE ROUGH HOUSE), an asylum for youth in Hamburg, Germany, which was established by an evangelical Pastor, Johann Hinrich Wichern, and soon served as a shelter for the homeless, for hungry and sick people, prostitutes and sailors. At the beginning of Advent a cross - the emblem of forgiveness – was erected, with four candles, one at each end, and lit progressively each Sunday. Later, this precursor of the wreath, perhaps because of the fire hazard, was replaced by a garland that was draped over a candelabra with four candles attached. Thus the wreath was born. The first candles were most likely white, later changed to red, the color of salvation. Red ribbons were attached to the wreath, and the whole contraption hung on a hook from the ceiling, again perhaps for reasons of safety, but also to allow the light to shine and illuminate the room.

The Advent wreath was very rich in Christian symbolism and so delightful and attractive that it soon became a fixture in common homes, although it may have been in churches first. And of course, what had a beginning in Europe, soon found its way across the ocean to the Americas and other continents. The making of the wreath is in many homes a highly anticipated event. In my home where I grew up, it was my Father's job, sometime between spring and fall, to cut a few slender, but sturdy shoots from hazelnut bushes, of which there was no short supply in our own forest. These my Mom would soak in warm water for several days to make them pliable, then shape them into a ring, tying the ends solidly together. This was the foundation of the wreath. When the Advent season approached, usually on the Saturday before the first of Advent, it was again my Dad or my older siblings and later myself, who would go out into the forest and bring home spruce or fir branches. The whole family would then be engaged in cutting sprigs, handing them to my Mom, who was the "official" wreath-maker. With plenty of greens and twine, the circle would quickly take shape. Long red ribbons would then be wound around the wreath at four symmetrical places and the appropriate lengths tied together at the top. Between the four ribbons, four candle holders (made of metal), into which the candles were inserted, would be securely fastened to the wreath. Before candle holders were machine-made and store-bought, wire was used. Even nowadays wreaths could be made at home, especially where there are children; loose greens can be purchased in many stores. For us it was always a wonderful experience, filled with anticipation.

The lighting of the candles each Sunday is a deeply moving event, in which the whole family participates. It is a time of reflection and devotion, but also of joy, doing crafts and making presents for each other or relatives and friends, of telling and sharing stories, reading poetry, making music and singing songs and carols, although Christmas carols are to be saved for that glorious celebration: Christmas Eve, Christmas Day and the following weeks.

ANGELS

Angels are messengers of God and defenders of humanity. As such they have always played a significant role in the relationship between God and man, as well as in some extra ordinary events like the destruction of Sodom and Gomorrah as executioners of God's will and punishment.

Angels are created, celestial, spiritual beings, in dignity a little higher than man, and the title, SONS OF GOD, is considered to be a reference to angels. They are divided into ten groups: Archangels, angels, seraphim, cherubim, principalities, authorities, powers, thrones, might and dominion. These different ranks imply different degrees of power, authority and activity, i.e. ministry and glory.

In the Christmas story beginning at Luke 1, we encounter the angel Gabriel visiting the elderly priest, Zechariah, who was at the time on duty in the temple. The angel announced the birth of a son to his equally aged wife, Elizabeth. The boy was to be named **John**. Since his mother Elizabeth and Mary, the mother of Jesus were cousins, John and Jesus were likewise cousins and contemporaries. John's mission was to spiritually prepare the way for the coming of the Messiah, Jesus Christ, i.e. to prepare the people for Jesus' ministry.

When Elizabeth was in her sixth month pregnant, the angel Gabriel was again dispatched, this time to Mary with the news that she was chosen to be the Mother of the Son of God, to be overshadowed by the Holy Spirit and to give birth to a boy, who was to be named **Jesus**, which means **Saviour**. Since Mary and Joseph were at this time engaged, but not yet married, this was a problem for Joseph, and he was understandably disturbed (Matthew 1:18-24). The angel of the Lord appeared to him in a dream to confirm God's plan and to encourage him to wed Mary and accept responsibility for her and for Jesus, his foster son.

When Jesus Christ, the Saviour of the world, was born in Bethlehem in Judea, an angel of the Lord appeared to shepherds, who were keeping watch over their flocks in the night; while the glory of the Lord *shone around them*, the shepherds were filled with fear. The angel said to them, *"Be not afraid; for behold, I bring you good news of a great joy which will come to all the people; for to you is born this day in the city of David a Saviour, who is Christ the Lord. And this will be a sign for you: you will find a babe wrapped in swaddling cloths and lying in a manger." And suddenly there was with the angel a multitude of heavenly host praising God and saying, "Glory to God in the highest, and on earth peace among men with whom he is pleased!" And the angels went away into heaven.* (Luke 2:8-15)

The angel of the Lord was three more times the bearer of news: after the Wise Men had visited, presented their gifts and worshiped the child Jesus (now the Holy Family living in a house, according to Matthew 2:11), they were told not to return and report to Herod the king on their homeward journey; Joseph was warned in a dream to take Mary and the child and flee to Egypt, since Herod intended to destroy the newborn King, and again when it was safe to return, with further instructions.

The birth of Jesus Christ was an earth-shattering event, and humanity will never be the same. It should not come as a surprise, that from the beginning of the incarnation of God to the end of the story (although in some ways the story is unending because God's act of salvation is without end for as long as the earth exists in its present form), a multitude of angels was employed to help accomplish God's plan. It is not surprising then, that the Christmas season has produced a business of "angels" in a variety of shapes and forms: pictures, posters, figurines, on wrapping paper and gift boxes, cups and mugs, tree decoration and cards – the list is endless. Many of the displays are not of angels at all, but of puttes, ornamental images of winged children that look like angels, but have their origin in mythology. This production and fascination with angels is bordering on a cult. According to God's Word, angels are not to be venerated, worshiped or prayed to. They are our servants, but only through the intervention of God's good order. It is right and fitting that we should appreciate these godly, invisible heavenly hosts around us, which are sent to help, encourage and guard us, but our thanksgiving for them is directed to the Holy Trinity of God, their Creator and Him only.

There is a connection between the angels of paradise – bad news – and the angel of Christ's birth – good news: When Adam and Eve were cast out of the Garden of Eden because of their disobedience to God, angels were placed at the gate of paradise to hinder their re-entry. When Christ was born, the angel was sent to proclaim the good news that heaven was once again accessible through Him.

According to Hebrew tradition there are four archangels: Michael, Gabriel, Raphael and Uriel. However, the Old and New Testament only refer to Michael as Archangel and the defender of Israel. Gabriel has the distinctive role of messenger.

THE COLLECTED WORKS by Billy Graham – ANGELS provides invaluable information on this subject.

ANIMALS

Most nativity scenes, paintings and crèches include domestic animals, in particular an ox and an ass. These were animals of burden; the ox used for ploughing and other heavy work; the ass for carrying grain, fruit, lumber, people, etc. Neither the Gospel of Matthew, nor the Gospel of Luke, which give us fairly detailed accounts of the birth of Christ and the subsequent events, mention these animals as being present in the stable. So how did they get into this privileged position? Was it just the fancy of the artists, the imagination of the contemplatives or the writers to make the story more interesting? The evidence may come from the Book of Isaiah 1:3: *The ox knows its owner and the ass its master's crib; but Israel does not know, my people does not understand.* The prophet Isaiah was called into ministry by the Lord and to the kingdom of Judah in the year 740 B.C. (Isaiah 6:1), and although the book may have been written by three different authors, it is providing hundreds of predictions about the Messiah, Jesus Christ. Since all of these prophesies concerning Jesus' birth, ministry, suffering, death and resurrection have been fulfilled, it is very likely that the vision of domestic animals, an ox and an ass in the stable where Mary and Joseph sought shelter, came true also. Many depictions of the nativity include a host of house pets and wild animals like birds, dogs, sheep and later on with the visit of the Magi/Wise Men, possibly camels. According to the apostle Paul, not only mankind was waiting for a redeemer, but he says, *"We know that the whole creation has been groaning in travail together until now; and not only the creation, but we ourselves, who have the first fruits of the Spirit, groan inwardly as we wait for adoption as sons, the redemption of our bodies."* (Romans 8:22) This verse seems to indicate the legitimacy of animals present at the birth of the Saviour and the fulfillment of Isaiah's prophesy. The ass may also have been the property of Joseph, who was a carpenter by trade back in Nazareth, his hometown. He would have used the animal to carry lumber, stones and tools as he went about his work. The ass may have come in handy to carry supplies for the journey to Bethlehem and have offered a welcome relief for Mary to ride on, who was heavy with child.

ANNA
At the time of the Holy Family's visit to the temple in Jerusalem for the rite of purification, there was a prophetess by the name of Anna. She was eighty-four years old and never departed from the temple; she worshiped, fasted and prayed day and night. At her encounter with the Messiah (the baby Jesus) *she gave thanks to God and spoke of him to all who were looking for the redemption of Jerusalem* (Luke 2:36-38).

AUGUSTUS
Generally known as Octavian, Augustus became the first Roman Emperor called CAESAR. Since the Roman Empire extended over much of Europe, parts of Africa and Asia, including Palestine, the city of Bethlehem, the birthplace of Christ, was in his realm at that time. (Luke 2:1) When he called for a census to be taken, all the men had to go to the place of their birth to be enrolled. Thus it was that Joseph and Mary had to make the long trip to Bethlehem. The mighty Caesar Augustus was but a tiny figure in God's immense plan! Jesus, the co-creator of heaven and earth submitted to the earthly rule of the emperor to indicate that He had not come to be a political ruler, an earthly King, but that His Kingdom was of a spiritual nature.

BABY JESUS
No one makes it more clear than John, the Gospel writer, disciple of Christ and close friend, that in Jesus Christ *"God became flesh"*, He was Immanuel – God with us. A careful reading of the first chapter of John, verse 1-18, will reveal the deeply spiritual meaning of the birth and purpose of Christ. The angel announcing the birth to the shepherds said plainly, *"Be not afraid, for behold, I bring you good news of a great joy which will come to all the people; for you is born this day in the city of David a Saviour, who is Christ the Lord. And this will be a sign for you: you will find the babe wrapped in swaddling cloths and lying in a manger."* (Luke 2:10-12)

At Christmas we think, of course, of Jesus as a Baby; numerous stories and songs have been written about the infant, but He grew up to become a man, to teach us and reveal God's plan for us and ultimately to die for us on the cross, so that by our faith in Him we would have the forgiveness of our sins. The sole purpose of His incarnation was the redemption of mankind, a carefully executed plan of the Holy Trinity. To see only the babe and not the God in that infant is to see the manger without the shadow of the cross; the child Jesus did not deliver us from sin, but the man called Christ, did. He was sinless, but He gave Himself, like a lamb for a sacrifice, to atone for our wrongdoings. No Christmas can be celebrated without this recollection and meditation.

BAKING AND COOKING

To eat, drink and be merry was one of the commands of God to His people whenever there was an occasion for celebration. At times God's Word says, *do not be sad; do not weep*, as in Nehemiah 8:10-12.

Then He said to them, *"Go your way, eat the fat and drink the sweet wine and send portions to him for whom nothing is prepared; for this day is holy to the Lord; and do not be grieved, for the joy of the Lord is your strength." And all the people went their way to eat and drink and to send portions and to make great rejoicing, because they had understood the words that were declared to them.*

There cannot possibly be any greater celebration than that of Christmas! This was, and always will be, the birth of our Saviour! No matter how the world distorts the issue, the meaning and the joy, how it tries to cover up this divine event, it is the greatest joy that has come down to us from heaven! It would be an insult to God and all the heavenly hosts not to celebrate, not to be happy, to sing and make music, to dance and decorate, to cook and bake and to give gifts, but with great deliberation and consciousness of the reason, and with genuine generosity towards friends and neighbours. It may not be easy to shut out the noise of the secular world around us, to withstand its temptations to buy and over-indulge, to go into dept for the sake of the season; it takes a real effort to remain "still" in this time of busyness and excitement. Tasks like cooking and baking don't have to fall into the mire of stress and self-imposed obligations; with careful planning they can be incorporated into the preparation activities without infringement on the Christmas spirit and without harm to the festive mood.

Here is an easy recipe for **Marashino Eyes**:

250 g unbleached flour
1 tsp baking powder
75 g sugar

1 tsp vanilla
1 tsp lemon
grated peel of one lemon
1 pinch of salt
1 egg yoke
125 g unsalted butter
1 egg white, lightly beaten
Maraschino cherries

Sift flour and baking powder into medium size bowl, making a well in the centre. Add sugar, aromas, peel, salt and egg yoke; stir and mix some of the flour into this dough, cover with flour, add cubed, cold butter and knead into a smooth ball. Shape this into a roll, cut pieces off, the size of a walnut, place on a greased cookie sheet and flatten a bit, brush with beaten egg white. Press into the centre a piece of maraschino cherry or flatten with fork to make a flat cookie. Bake 10 min. at 160 C (325 F).

Note: Since every stove produces different temperatures, cookies have to be watched carefully while baking since they burn easily.

To have something nice on hand during this season for unexpected guests who suddenly drop in: **Chocolate-Peppermint loaf**:

225 g butter (room temperature)
250 g sugar, plus 2 tbsp.
4 eggs, large
2 tbsp. cocoa powder, heaped (high quality, 70 % or more)
2 tbsp. peppermint oil
1 tbsp. green food colouring
½ c water, plus 2 tbsp. (room temperature)
500 g unbleached flour, sifted
4 tsp. baking powder, sifted
1 tbsp. sifted icing sugar

Grease loaf pan, dust with bread crumbs. Heat oven to 175 C (350 F).
In large bowl, cream butter with some sugar, add eggs, one at a time, plus sugar. Cream well. Add half of the flour and baking powder, stir well. Add ½ c of water, stir until all the water is absorbed. Stir rest of flour into dough until smooth. Divide dough into three parts and place in different bowls. Into one part stir one

tbsp. of water. To the second part add one tbsp. of water, one tbsp. of sifted cocoa powder and one tbsp. of sugar. Mix well. To last part add peppermint oil and food colouring, plus last tbsp. of sugar. Mix until well blended. This part of the dough should have the same consistency as the others; it may be necessary to add a tbsp. of flour to achieve this. Add the peppermint dough and the chocolate dough to white dough, run a spoon or a fork <u>lightly</u> through all of them to create marbling effect. Spoon into loaf pan. Bake 50 min. Test the center with a wooden chopstick; if it comes out clean, the cake is done. If dough still clings to it, bake another 10 min. or so. Test again. When cake is done, let cool in pan for 20 min., then slip onto cooling wire, board or plate. When cold, dust with icing sugar. Enjoy!

For alternative recipe: Leave all the dough white, just add ¾ c chocolate chips and ¾ c mint chips.

BELLS

According to Webster's Dictionary, a bell is a metallic, hollow device that vibrates and gives forth a ringing sound when struck. The making and use of bells goes back thousands of years; it is supposed to have been fashioned and used in China and India since 9000 B.C. The Old Testament mentions bells only in reference to the embellishment of the priests robes, in particular their fringes (Exodus 28:34; 39:26).

These bells may have acted as signs of attention that the priest who offered the sacrifices, which could be lengthy in time, was in the Holy of Holies and that he was still alive. Zechariah the prophet mentions bells in connection with Christ's reign in Jerusalem (Second Coming): *At the festival of shelters, even the horses will carry bells on their harnesses, inscribed, "Dedicated to the Lord"* (Zechariah 14:20). There is no reference to bells in the New Testament. Yet, especially at Christmas time pictures of bells are everywhere: on posters, greeting cards, made of paper mache and tinfoil, wax and real metals, hanging from lanterns in the streets, in stores, as house and home decorations – bells unlimited!

The making of bells is an art form; they are made in a foundry usually of an alloy consisting of different metals, mostly copper and zinc. The molten metals are mixed, then poured into a cast that has been specifically made. The size and the alloy determines the tone. The right amount of each metal and the right measurement are extremely important in the casting of a bell, if it is to harmonize with others already in existence at the same place.

While most churches, at least the older ones, have bells, they seldom ring them in North America. The reasons may be manifold: The churches old structures cannot withstand the stress of these swinging colossuses; by-laws against noise pollution; a lack of trained bell ringers, or a congregation may simply have outgrown its use. But you would not want to miss the happy cacophony of these implements singing and ringing in any town or city in Europe on a Saturday night or Sunday morning. In most countries, at 18 o'clock on a Saturday evening, the bells begin to peal to indicate the close of the work week and to usher in the Sunday. This is a happy moment of silence and reflection for many people, an opportunity to stop and enter a day, a phase of rest. Sunday morning the bells toll to wake up the worshipers and to call them to early Mass, and all morning long they ring and call as people attend different services at different times and locations.

Since modern technology is providing mankind with exact time and up-dated news on a regular basis, a very vital function of the bells in the modern world has almost completely vanished: the bell as a herald of tidings – good or bad. Many churches have more than one bell; each has a different sound and meaning, but even where there is only one bell, the way it is rung gives explicit information to those who hear its sound. Apart from calls to worship and prayer, the bell would announce the start of the day, midday and the close of the day. It would be further used to announce the birth of a child, some ones death, or a sudden calamity, like fire, where all hands were needed to come and help. This use is still the case in rural communities and outlying areas in Europe. Because of the bells resonance, the message is carried high and far through the air to deliver important news. Whoever is familiar with the writings of Friedrich Schiller (1759-1805), will most likely know the poem called THE BELL, the depiction of life from birth to death, accompanied by the ringing of the bell.

It is no wonder that bells have become the symbol of good tidings at Christmas: Jesus Christ is born, the Messiah has come, Emmanuel – God with us!

BETHLEHEM

The name Bethlehem means House of Bread; it was a village in the hill country of Judah, also called Ephrat at the time of Jacob. Here, Jacob buried his beloved Rachel, who had died giving birth to Benjamin, the youngest of what was to become the "twelve tribes of Judah". Bethlehem is mentioned again in the Book of Ruth: Ruth was born in Moab, she left her country with Naomi, her mother-in-law, to settle in Bethlehem, Naomi's former home. Here Ruth meets and marries a wealthy landowner by the name of Boaz; their son Obed becomes the father of Jesse and grandfather of David. When David was a young lad, tending his fathers' flocks in the fields around Bethlehem, the prophet Samuel was sent by God to anoint David as future king of Israel. He spent some apprentice years in the house of Saul, his predecessor, before being elected to the throne. Now the stage was set for a few prophesies to be fulfilled:

There shall come forth a shoot from the stump of Jesse, and a branch shall grow out of his roots. And the spirit of the Lord shall rest upon him, the spirit of wisdom and understanding, the spirit of counsel and might, the spirit of knowledge and the fear of the Lord. And his delight shall be in the fear of the Lord. (Isaiah 11:1-3a)

For to us a child is born, to us a son is given; and the government will be upon his shoulder, and his name will be called "Wonderful Counselor, Mighty God, Everlasting Father, Prince of Peace." Of the increase of his government and of peace there will be no end, upon the throne of David, and over his kingdom, to establish it, and to uphold it with justice and with righteousness from this time forth for evermore. The zeal of the Lord of hosts will do this. (Isaiah 9:6-7)

But you, O Bethlehem Ephratha, who are little to be among the clans of Judah, from you shall come forth for me one who is to be ruler in Israel, whose origin is from of old, from ancient days. (Micah 5:2)

Because of these prophesies Bethlehem was looked upon as the place where the Messiah would be born, but when He was, no one looked or listened, no one knew, no welcome was prepared for Him. The angel gave God's message of the birth of Christ to the shepherds, these passed it on to the folks in town on their way back to their herds; God announced this tremendous news to the Wise Men in the East and guided them by a star to Bethlehem to the newborn King, to pay homage, to worship Him, to present gifts as was customary for Royalty, but King Herod in nearby Jerusalem and his personnel, did not know; the religious leaders of the country did not know. *He was in the world, and the world was made through him, yet the world knew him not. He came to his own home, and his own people received him not.*

(John 1:10-11) It is God's good pleasure to choose what is small, humble and insignificant to fulfill His purposes.

BIBLE

The Bible is the Holy Word of God and consists of the Old Testament and the New Testament. By the fourth century A.D. the main texts of Judaism and the writings about the life of Christ had been combined in one book to make it easier for the Christian Church and believers to read and help propagate the faith. Here are documented the faithful works of God, from the beginning of creation to the establishment of the Nation Israel and its history, the many prophetic references to the coming of the Messiah, Jesus Christ, His suffering, death and resurrection. New Testament writings give witness to the beginning and growth of the Christian Church, as well as its persecutions. It is a tradition that in every Christian church and in millions of homes the Gospel (good news) of the Nativity is read on Christmas Eve or Christmas Day; it reminds us again what this season is all about: not the gifts we give, but the gift God gave in His Son for our salvation.

BOXING DAY

Predominantly in the British Commonwealth, the 26th of December was declared a legal holiday, and on this day boxed gifts were presented to the servants. In most other European countries it is a legal holiday too, but considered the **Second Day of Christmas**, usually used to pay visits or spend leisurely with the children and friends in games or outdoor activities.

While in the U.S.A. it is business as usual on this day; in Canada, the 26th of December or BOXING DAY, is often the busiest day of the month. Gifts and merchandise are returned or exchanged at stores, and many shops have special sales prices at this time to cash in on the holiday mood and spending. Some businesses have gone so far as not to deal with the return of gifts on this day at all, but only serve customers with the sale of goods, dealing with other matters in the following days. This has proven to be beneficial to both, stores and customers alike. However, the meaning of Boxing Day has vastly changed from its initial use to contemporary practice, just like so many other traditions.

CANDLE MASS (see PURIFICATION)

CANDLES

"One small candle dispels the darkness" is an old saying. There is hardly anyone alive in the world who hasn't had the occasion to run for a candle and matches during a power failure! The Advent and Christmas season is almost unthinkable without the flickering light and the sweet smell of candles. However we may use them: on the Advent wreath, on the tree, on the coffee table or in the church, the real purpose of their light is the reference to JESUS CHRIST as THE LIGHT OF THE WORLD. In the Gospel of John (1:4-5, 9) we read these words: *In him was life and the life was the light of man. The light shines in the darkness, and the darkness has not overcome it. The true light that enlightens every man was coming into the world.* Christmas is truly the FESTIVAL OF LIGHT.

Candles are as ancient as time. They were first made from bees wax and tallow, with a cotton wick to absorb the wax and burn it. Oil with a wick coiled in a container was also an early means of producing light. Later on, candles were made of paraffin, a waxy, chrystalline substance, distilled from wood, coal and other sources. At first, most candles had an off-white shade; those that were used to lighten a Christmas tree would be securely placed in a holder made from wire, which was carefully attached to a branch, away from other branches so as not to catch fire. This was always done with great care. Manufacturers soon produced colored candles: red, blue, gold, yellow, pink, etc. to create a greater show for the eye and perfumed candles with aromas like cinnamon, pine, winterberry, allspice, etc. as well as special holders. Candles on the tree have been replaced with electric lights, if possible, for greater safety and durability, and these again come in white or colored.

Where I was born and lived the first ten years of my life, we had no electricity. Petroleum lamps were used for household and barn chores on winter evenings. On the Advent wreath and on the Christmas tree candles were used, but a pail of water was never far away! Electric lights are a wonderful invention, and we wouldn't want to be without them, but they can never replace the shimmer of a flickering light in the eye of a loved one, the physical and emotional warmth and the romantic sense candles exude. The burning wick, silently consuming itself, holds a mysterious fascination that is hard to describe. A lighted candle is a living thing and seems to tell a story; it represents mortality, but tells the story of hope for immortality with Christ.

CAROLS

Was it the first Christmas carol at the birth of Jesus? *And suddenly there was with the angel a multitude of the heavenly host praising God and saying, "Glory to God in the highest, and on earth peace among men with whom he is pleased!"* (Luke 2:13-14)

As the angels disappeared into heaven, and the shepherds went and spread the word of all they had heard and seen before resuming their jobs in the fields to watch their flocks, others took up their praises to God. And they never stopped. And they never will. And they never should, for the birth of Jesus is the greatest deed God has ever done. I hear critics shouting: the greatest deed was done on Calvary! But think: Would there have been a Calvary if there had not been a Bethlehem?

The Gospel accounts do not tell us whether there was music in the spheres on that Holy Night, but I like to think there was. If *the morning stars sang together, and all the sons of God shouted for joy* at the time of creation (Job 38:7), would they not have had more reason at the birth of the Saviour? Millions of pens have scribbled prose and poetry, lyrics and music, carols and songs, describing His birth; millions of voices have repeated the angels' refrain and the prophet's word: *For to us a child is born, to us a son is given.* (Isaiah 9:6) I may never be able to compose a JOY TO THE WORLD or SILENT NIGHT, but I too can lift my voice in praise and adoration, just like the poor shepherds did.

CHRIST

ANOINTED in Greek; THE ANOINTED ONE, equal to the title of MESSIAH in Hebrew and Aramaic, King of Israel. The name CHRIST is almost always used in connection with Jesus (Saviour), the name given Him at the annunciation by the angel of the Lord (Luke 1:31). He was the Saviour, the connecting link between God and humanity; at the same time He was a priest, *For it was witnessed of him, "Thou art a priest for ever, after the order of Melchizedek."* (Hebrews 7:17) Not only was He priest whose function was sacrificial on behalf of the people, but He gave Himself as a sacrifice, being both, the High Priest and the Sacrificial Lamb. In Isaiah 9, other titles are bestowed on Christ: *For to us a child is born, to us a son is given; and the government will be upon his shoulder, and his name will be called "Wonderful Counselor, Mighty God, Everlasting Father, Prince of Peace."* (Isaiah 9:6) From the name CHRIST, the religious movement called CHRISTIANITY, has derived its name, as well as a number of commemorations, holidays and things, but mostly those associated with Christmas.

CHRISTIANITY AND THE CHRISTIAN CHURCH

The founder of Christianity was Jesus Christ, the Son of God. By His teachings, His life, death, resurrection and ascension and ultimately the outpouring of the Holy Spirit at Pentecost, He had sown the seed and built the foundation for the Christian Church. The first time the name CHURCH is mentioned in the Bible is in the New Testament, Matthew 16:18, where Jesus says, *"And I tell you, you are Peter, and on this rock I will build my church, and the powers of death shall not prevail against it."* From the first congregation of eleven, plus a substitute for Judas Iscariot, who had betrayed the Lord (and then killed himself), and a few women, in a short time after the resurrection it had grown to 120, and on Pentecost 3000 souls were added (Acts 1:15; 2:41). Thus began the Christian Church.

Because Christ had commissioned and empowered Peter to be the head of the Church, he is seen as the first Bishop or Pope. Although Peter had evangelized and was martyred in Rome, the Office of the Church took some time to be fully established. There were great persecutions of new believers throughout Asia and Europe, until the Emperor Constantine himself in the fourth century accepted the Christian faith and granted religious freedom in his realm to others so inclined. A study of the history of Christianity and the Church reveals many changes, a sign that it is not static, but alive, working, growing and maturing into perfection when Christ will come again. (More under CHURCH)

CHRISTMAS

CHRIST'S MASS, also called THE LITURGY OF THE NATIVITY. The birth date of Jesus Christ is unknown. Since it is documented that king Herod the Great of Judah died in 4 B.C., and since he persecuted the infant newborn King and massacred all the children two years and younger in Bethlehem and surrounding area in order to kill Jesus, the latter would have been born before that date. Thus we know that our present-day calendar, which was designed to begin with the year of Christ's birth, is off by several years. Both, the 25th of December (the solstice) and the 6th of January were pagan holidays. In order to help the general populace to accept Christianity, the Feast of the Nativity on the 25th

was introduced. In the East, Christmas began to be observed with a three-fold emphasis: The visit of the Wise Men, the Baptism of the Lord and the first miracle at Cana. Thus the whole of the Western Church celebrates Christmas on December 25th; the Eastern (Orthodox) Church on January 7th (the 6th of January is Christmas Eve).

Thousands of Biblical scholars, theologians and astronomers have researched scripture and other ancient manuscripts in order to determine the exact date of Jesus' birth, but have always come up short. Maybe we can get a bit closer to the real date: What if God, in that particular year, used HANUKKAH, the Feast of Dedication, i.e. the re-dedication of the temple after it was cleansed by Judas Maccabeus from pollution by Antiochus Epiphanes (The Book of Maccabees in the Apocrypha of the Bible), which is also called the Celebration of Light, for His Son's birth? Jews believe that a miracle took place at that time. There was no oil to be found anywhere in Jerusalem or all of Israel to re-ignite the light in the temple, which was supposed to never extinguish. While removing the accumulated rubbish and cleaning every nook and cranny, a small flask of oil was discovered, the light was lit and burned for three days, when fresh supplies were available. Jesus Christ was (and is) the light that came into the world to save it. We know that God loves symbolism; the Bible is full of examples. Might He have sent His Son into the world as light on the day of the Festival of Lights? It may seem far-fetched, but is it? Let us look at some other occurences. First, Christ was crucified on the day of preparation for the Passover; all over Israel lambs were slaughtered for that feast. (See Matthew 27:26-31); Mark 15:14-15; Luke 23:22-23; John 19:13-19) On the cross, Jesus was killed for the sins of the world. As the blood of the lambs on the lintels of the houses of the Israelites in Egypt (See Exodus 12) saved them from losing their first-born, the blood of God's first-born was shed for our salvation. Second, fifty days after the resurrection of Jesus Christ, on a Feast Day called Pentecost (fiftieth day after Passover), a Jewish Festival, THE FEAST OF HARVEST (First- fruits), was celebrated. It was later called SHABUOTH and given another meaning: a commemoration of the revelation of the Ten Commandments at Mount Sinai. It was God's choice to pour out the Holy Spirit on this Feast Day. In each case God had given the direction for these celebrations, and now, at the birth of the Christian Church He used them again to make a point: Salvation through Christ (Good Friday and Easter) and regeneration through the Holy Spirit (Pentecost). (See Exodus 12:7-13; Acts 2)

But even if we would know for a fact that Jesus was born on Hanukkah, the exact date would still elude us, and that was precisely what God wanted: obscurity, modesty, humility. Not the date, not the festival to be important, but the object: JESUS CHRIST. As most Jewish holidays are determined by the phase of the moon, the date of the Festival of Hanukkah, like most others, is flexible, but usually falls into December, at a season of the year when it is darkest on the earth (at least in the Northern hemisphere where Israel is located); Christ was born at a time when the Jewish Nation sat, spiritually and politically, in great darkness.

In North America, as can be expected, immigrants and settlers took their own traditions and celebrations to the place of their choice and added new traditions, depending on location and circumstances, but the meaning remained the same all over the world: the birth of Jesus Christ, the Saviour. Unfortunately, through over-emphasis on gift-giving and hoopla, the real package is often hard to find amidst boxes, wrappings, ribbons and debts. It can be a challenge to shift the focus from the commerce of the holidays to, as someone has said, the **Reason for the Season**.

CHRISTMAS CAKE

This is a controversial subject: Some people love it, others hate it. There are perhaps a dozen or more recipes, but all use an abundance and variety of nuts and fruits, especially green and red maraschino cherries. It is usually baked early in the season and soaked with rum or whisky, and this is ignited when served. If children are present, the alcohol is omitted. Stories about Christmas cake abound, from using it as a bookend, a door stopper or to ward off starvation, and you may add yours if you have one*. In recent years, Christmas cakes from other countries have made their appearance on North American scenes: the English Plum Pudding, the German Stollen, the Italian Panettone, for example. Christmas gives us a wonderful opportunity to try out our own traditions as well as others.

*The story, **A Christmas Memory** by Truman Capote (1925-1984) is a thought-provoking description of the physical efforts and emotional involvement that sometimes go into the making of a Christmas cake!

CHURCH

When we hear the word "Church", we usually think of a building that is used for the gathering of the faithful in worship, prayer, Bible School, etc. This it is, for sure, but basically it means "The Body of Christ", made up of people who believe in Him and follow His doctrines. The Christian Church was founded by Christ, propagated by the disciples turned apostles and missionaries and is a vibrant, living religion in the world. Its establishment and growth can be likened to a tree: The Christian Church has its roots in Judaism: Jesus was the Son of God, which gave Him His divine nature, and the Son of Man, providing the human nature through His mother, a Jewish maiden. The birth of Christ, His atoning work on the cross, His burial for three days and subsequent resurrection, were planned and foretold by God through His prophets immediately after the fall in the Garden of Eden (Genesis 3:15). Hundreds of scripture passages in the Old Testament reveal this future rescue operation, which began the night Christ was born in Bethlehem. Much of what the Church is today is based on God's Word in the Old

Testament, for God did not change; His Word is true and stands forever and ever. What did change was, that sacrifices were no longer necessary, because Jesus had offered Himself as a living sacrifice, for all sin, for all times. What is necessary though is a living faith in Him; not an intellectual belief, but a heart trust in His power, mercy and grace. The apostle Paul expressed it this way: *"For by grace you have been saved through faith, and this is not your own doing, it is the gift of God – not because of works, lest any man should boast"* (Ephesians 2:8-9)

From the roots sprang the tree, growing and expanding. It took a few hundred years for the Church to hammer out guidelines of faith and formats of worship; many scholars and religious people worked diligently to interpret scripture properly, and it took many more missionaries to spread the Good News of the Gospel of Jesus Christ. By the turn of the millennium, the Christian Church was well established in Europe, parts of Asia and North Africa, but a schism started to develop over pontifical and doctrinal issues that split the Church in 1054 A.D. into two factions: The Western/Roman Catholic Church and the Eastern/Orthodox Church. By the fifteenth century the Roman Catholic Church had become very corrupt in its doctrines, teachings and administrations. While the general populace was mainly unaware of these errors because of illiteracy and Mass being said not in the common language of the country, but always in Latin, numerous religious and scholastic people worked diligently to bring about a reformation. To no avail. John Hus, a Roman Catholic priest in Czechoslovakia in the 15th century was burned at the stake as a heretic for his efforts to renew the teachings of the Church. Martin Luther, a German priest who likewise tried to regenerate the Church in 1517, was excommunicated, defrocked by Rome and a warrant was issued for his arrest – dead or alive. While God and friends rescued him and placed him under voluntary house arrest at Warthburg Castle in Germany, he spent the time translating the Bible into the common German language. In the meantime, the avalanche of renewal gained momentum and could not be stopped. Thousands protested against Rome; contemporaries like Calvin in France, Zwingli in Switzerland, Erasmus in the Netherlands, and numerous others in England were also toiling on reform. After ten months in hiding, Luther emerged, the Reformation took hold; whole congregations converted to what was quickly dubbed "Lutheranism" and new churches sprang up all over Europe. Another major break happened in 1534 when Henry the 8th broke with Rome and declared himself head of the Church of England, also called the Anglican Church. Here Wycliff and Tyndale had already done reformatory work. Since then, countless other denominations were established: The Mennonites, the Baptists, the Reformed Church, the Pentecostal Church and numerous free evangelical churches all over the world. The tree is **still** branching out and growing.

CIRCUMCISION

As a sign of God's covenant with Abram, He commanded him to circumcise every male born to him or in his household eight days after birth, or at any age retroactive, thus Abraham circumcised himself at the age of ninety-nine. Together with this covenant God changed Abram's name to Abraham. This command came after the birth of Ishmael and before the birth of Isaac (Genesis 17:1-14; 21:1-4).

The word, circumcision, is Latin for 'a cutting around'. The act consists of removing the foreskin of the penis and can be performed by the father of the child, a male relative, or in modern times by a professional (Mohel). Although this act is usually performed by a male, there was apparently no rule against a female taking the initiative to undertake this operation in case of urgency. In the fourth chapter of Exodus, verses 24-26, a surprising development makes this act necessary. We read, *At a lodging place on the way the Lord met him (Moses) and sought to kill him. Then Zipporah took a flint and cut off her son's foreskin, and touched Moses' feet with it, and said, "Surely you are a bridegroom of blood to me!" So He let him alone. Then it was that she said, "You are a bridegroom of blood", because of the circumcision.* Other translations claim that Zipporah touched his legs, still others that she held the foreskin against his genitals. The entire story is a mystery: Why would God want to kill Moses, whom He had just called and assigned to deliver the people of Israel? Perhaps either he or his son was not yet circumcised, or perhaps both, and was therefore not covered by the covenant between God and Abraham. A circumcision of Moses would not have been convenient at this time for health reasons, since a time of recuperation was needed. Moses and Aaron, his brother, were on an urgent mission to go back to Egypt, while the family stayed behind.

Jesus was circumcised at the end of eight days, at which time He was named JESUS, the name given by the angel Gabriel before He was conceived in the womb (Luke 2:21). Mary, the mother, would have been present, since this act did not have to be performed at the temple or synagogue.

CONCEPTION

The conception of Jesus was accomplished through the Holy Spirit – the Spirit of God – as announced to Mary by the angel Gabriel. The Apostle's Creed in its second part says, "I believe in Jesus Christ, His only Son, our Lord. He was conceived by the power of the Holy Spirit and born of the Virgin Mary." The Nicene Creed phrases it slightly different, "We believe in one Lord, Jesus Christ, the only Son of God, eternally begotten of the Father, God from God, Light from Light, true God from true God, begotten, not made, of one Being with the Father." The Athanasian Creed formulates the belief about the conception of Jesus with these words, "It is necessary for eternal salvation that one also faithfully believe that our Lord Jesus Christ became flesh. For this is the true faith that we believe and confess: That our Lord Jesus Christ, God's Son, is both God and man. He is God, begotten before all worlds from being of the Father, and He is man, born in the world from the being of His mother – existing fully as God, and fully as man with a rational soul and a human body; equal to the Father in divinity, subordinate to the Father in humanity. Although He is God and man, He is not divided, but is one Christ." (LBW – Min. Desk Ed.)

The conception of Christ is sometimes called "miraculous" because it was accomplished supernaturally through the Holy Spirit, not by man. (This concept is easier to understand if one accepts the fact that God is **Almighty** who, through His wisdom and power, created the heavens and the earth and everything in it and the universe around it.) The angel of the Lord himself said, "For with God nothing will be impossible." (Luke 1:37)

CONTEMPLATION

The word, "contemplation", is not often used in the English language; first, I think, it is sometimes substituted for "meditation", which is not the same. Second, it is understood to be part of the devotion of members of a religious order, like nuns, monks and priests, but unattainable to the average person or Christian. Third, most people never acquire the love or skill for this exercise. Like any skill, perfection comes with experience. So, what exactly is contemplation? Let WEBSTER speak: 1a) Concentration on spiritual things as a form of private devotion; 1b) a state of mystical awareness of God's Being; 2) an act of considering with attention, study; 3) the act of regarding steadily; 4) intention, expectation. There you have it! But now the question is how to do it. Since the topic of this book is CHRISTMAS, let's start there. Here are a few very simple suggestions:

- Select a time that is free from distractions.
- Shut out or switch off any noise.
- Chose a comfortable chair.
- Sit for a few minutes with eyes closed; listen and recognize some of the noises that can't be controlled, like the hum of the refrigerator, a dog barking outside, or the traffic under your window. Acknowledge these noises as normal, accept them and forget them.
- Think about what you would like to achieve: peace of mind, closeness to God, an experience of the meaning of Christmas, etc.
- Say a simple prayer: Lord, please forgive me all my sins, bring peace and healing to my soul. Open my mind to understand Your Word and my heart to receive it. Amen.
- Slowly, carefully read one of the Nativity stories in the Gospel of Matthew, Luke or John. For this exercise I recommend Luke 2:1-20. If some passage peaks your interest, stop there. Place yourself in that situation: perhaps the

difficult journey from Nazareth to Bethlehem, over the hills and through deep valleys, fording streams, in good and inclement weather. Mary, heavy with child, Joseph burdened with the awesome responsibility for this situation. Or perhaps you can identify more with the shepherds in a field at night, overwhelmed and frightened by the appearance of an angel with his fantastic news of God's Son born in town, this incredible invitation to go and see, then seeing a multitude of the heavenly hosts in the night sky, praising God in the Highest! See and listen with the shepherds! Go, run with them to Bethlehem, see the Babe, lying in a manger, wrapped in swaddling cloths. Stay awhile. Bend the knee. Adore. Worship. This Child is your Creator and Saviour!

You will gently come out of this experience refreshed, peaceful, in a normal, natural way, as if awakening from sleep, but the memory will never leave you; it will enrich your life and give you a new perspective on the Christmas event, and a new desire to celebrate differently, with more meaning. And, "If at first you don't succeed, try, try again!" However, this experience **must not** be confused with a trance; it is a devout, religious, spiritual exercise: this is CONTEMPLATION. We can thank Ignatius of Loyola for teaching us!

CRAFTS

The Advent and Christmas season is an ideal time for crafting. Winter evenings are long, anxiety mounts, and young children can draw and colour, glue-on felt pictures or cut snowflakes out of paper with blunt scissors. Older ones may be encouraged to create a Nativity scene with figures made from play dough or real bread dough (the latter lightly brushed with a mixture of egg yoke and water and briefly baked in the oven at light temperature – with supervision!) Sticks and stones, rocks, cones and evergreen sprigs can be creatively used to assemble a stable and surrounding fields. This is also an ideal time to tell or read the Christmas story to ensure that children know the meaning of this special time of year. Their fantasy will do the rest!

CRÈCHE

The word CRÈCHE is French for manger, but is often used as a whole representation of the Nativity scene. Complete sets can be purchased or individual pieces of the figurines acquired and the stable hand-made. It is more fun, however, if the entire scene is crafted, where all members of the family can contribute. It can be made of stones, wood, paper, or any other material flexible for shaping objects. Many a home has a crèche in honour of the Christ Child, and some traditions leave the manger vacant until midnight Christmas Eve or early Christmas morning, when the infant Jesus is placed in its crib for greater emphasis.

DAVID

By the 11th century B.C., the nation of Israel had become very populous; it had been given individual leaders by God like Moses, Aaron and Joshua, later it was ruled by Judges. But influenced by other nations around them, the people had taken their focus off God and clamoured for a king, seeing it as an ideal situation that apparently afforded safety, security and prosperity. God answered their request by having the prophet Samuel anoint Saul of Kish, from the tribe of Benjamin, at a chance meeting, as the first king of Israel. It's a tragic story of ineptness, failed successes, illness and despair. Having to deal with the neighbouring Philistines, who regularly came in to ruin cities, plunder goods and people and steal or destroy harvests, Saul crumbled under the weight of the crown's responsibility. His bouts with depressions made the matter worse. To cheer him up, a young lad by the name of David was hired to play music to the king to lift his spirits. Unbeknownst to Saul, David was already chosen and anointed to become the future king of Israel.

God was well aware that under Saul's leadership Israel was like a herd of sheep without a shepherd. Again He summoned the prophet Samuel to go to Bethlehem to a man named Jesse who had eight sons. One of these Samuel was to anoint king. This was done without the knowledge of Saul and under the pretense that Samuel had gone to sacrifice and worship the Lord at an existing altar in the area. As one after the other passed muster before Samuel, from the eldest to the youngest present, God indicated to the prophet that none of these was chosen. *And Samuel said to Jesse, "Are all your sons here?" And he said, "There remains yet the youngest, but behold he is keeping the sheep." And Samuel said to Jesse, send and fetch him; for we will not sit down till he comes here."* (1. Samuel 16:11) To the surprise of all, David was anointed to become, in time, the second king of Israel, although this was wrapped strictly in secrecy. When king Saul was once again suffering from illness, which was diagnosed as depression or an *evil spirit*, David was called and brought to sing and make music in order to lift the king's mood. It was so pleasing to Saul that he requested to keep the young man at his court. This was David's apprenticeship and preparation for his future reign. After Saul's death, David was made king of Judah, and after seven and a half years he was also made king of Israel and reigned a total of forty years. Through the prophet, Nathan, God gave David a promise, *"And your house and your kingdom shall be made sure for ever before me; your throne shall be established for ever."* (2. Samuel 7:16) This was God's plan for the Messiah to come out of the stem of Jesse, through the line of David and to be born in Bethlehem. Here the genealogies of Matthew (1:1-17) and Luke (3:23-38) are very helpful to trace Christ's ancestry.

DECORATIONS

Records show that the earliest decorations for the Christmas season were like those used for the pagan holidays of Saturnalia and Janus: Evergreens, berries and flowers from nature. These old festivals began on the 17th of December and lasted well into January, a time when the sun's orbit was low in the sky and daylight was short, when little outdoor work could be done – at least in the Northern hemisphere – and spring and summer were a long way off. To counter the "blaaahs" of winter, people decorated their homes with greenery, with hemlock, fir, spruce, pine, cedar, juniper or holly, as a reminder of new life, a sign of hope for the new year, new seedtime and harvest and new prosperity. They ate and drank, danced and feasted as much as their often meagre purses allowed. The mistletoe was also a beloved indoor decoration, and not only in England, but also in Northern Germany and Scandinavia. A sprig would usually be fastened on the lintel of a doorway to signal peace. When the custom of "kissing under the mistletoe" was first introduced, is not clear; Dickens writes about it in his LONDONER SKETCHES.

As the 25th of December was declared by the Roman Church as the official chosen date of Christ's birth and named CHRISTMAS, in private many of the old festivals and traditions were simply transferred to the new reality. To be sure, for many centuries pagan traditions were observed alongside Christian customs. Old habits are hard to break!

Decorations for this season vary enormously, according to religious fervour, cultural background and family traditions.

DOVE

One of the frequent and popular symbols of Christmas is the dove. Most commonly, it is associated with peace; after all, didn't the angels declare peace on earth? Yes and no! They announced *"peace on earth among men with whom he* (God) *is pleased!"* Since Adam and Eve, since Cain and Abel, there has been sin and violence. And although Jesus Christ has conquered sin and death through His death on the cross, His resurrection and ascension into heaven, where He is seated at the right hand of the Father, peace on earth can only happen where there is genuine good will among people. Only when Jesus returns to rule the world will there be real peace. How then did the dove become the symbol of peace? There are several stories in the Bible where the dove figures prominently, including the Christmas story. But we begin with Noah: When the waters of the flood were subsiding, Noah sent out a dove on a reconnaissance flight; it came back with a green olive leaf in its beak. A week later he sent it out again, and it did not return, it had found dry land. The story of the flood and God's saving grace to Noah, his family and all the animals, has always been intertwined with the Christmas story: God's desire is to save, not to destroy.

The dove has been used in early Christianity to depict the Holy Spirit, the Third Person of the Godhead. Hundreds of artists have used this symbol to capture the annunciation of the Angel Gabriel to Mary: The Holy Spirit in the form of a dove alighting on the Blessed Virgin to indicate the miraculous conception. We encounter the dove again at the time of the purification ritual, where two doves were sacrificed. Because the dove was adopted as the symbol of the Holy Spirit, we find it prominently displayed in our churches, on stained glass windows, vestments, paintings, in Christian books, cards, etc., even on gravestones. It is especially used at Pentecost and Trinity Sundays, but also at baptisms and confirmations.

EGYPT

Israel's association with Egypt goes back thousands of years to the time of Abram, though Israel as a nation did not yet exist. When Jacob, grandson of Abraham, returned from his ancestors country, where he got married and accumulated much wealth, on the journey he was faced by a man, who turned out to be God Himself, that is, Christ, before He became flesh. As they wrestled together, Jacob won by perseverance, and the man asked him his name. *Then he said, "Your name shall no more be called Jacob, but Israel, for you have striven with God and with man, and have prevailed."* (Genesis 32:25-29) Through Joseph, one of the twelve sons of Jacob, who was sold as a slave by his brothers to a caravan travelling to Egypt and ultimately became Pharaoh's right hand and because of a famine in their land, his brothers were invited to settle in Egypt. They multiplied rapidly, and four hundred years later, after being enslaved by the Egyptians, were led out by the hand of God and a leader called MOSES. They settled in Canaan. Egypt continued to play major roles politically. At the time of the birth of Christ, much of Europe and Asia were occupied by Rome, with governors or kings ruling over the land. King Herod was entrusted with Judah where Bethlehem was located. When Joseph, the husband of Mary, was told in a dream to flee with her and the baby because Herod wanted to kill Jesus (he was jealous for his throne), God told him to go to Egypt. It was safe, not too far and relatively easy to get to because of the trade route, which they may have taken for safety reasons, where they could mingle with caravans.

EPIPHANY

The word Epiphany means appearance, manifestation and refers to Jesus' birth, but is in general understood to mean the appearing of the Wise Men from the East to visit the Christ Child in Bethlehem. The 6th of January is the Feast Day of this celebration. The Orthodox Church has made this holiday its Christmas Eve, while for the rest of the Christian world, Christmas officially ends with the 5th of January, even though the visit of the Wise Men has always been seen as part of the season. But there is a shift in the story; with the Wise Men leaving to go home, there is an immediate and dramatic change in the peaceful setting in Bethlehem: with Joseph being warned in a dream to take Mary and the Child and flee to Egypt, the Holy Family sets out without delay to escape the fury of king Herod. The whole story can be read in the Gospel of Matthew (chapter 2).

In some denominations and traditions, the baptism of the Lord and His first miracle in Cana are also commemorated on the Feast Day of Epiphany.

FRANKINCENSE

Frankincense is the second gift mentioned that is given to Jesus by the Wise Men. It is the fragrant resin of gum trees, especially boswellia sacra, which grew predominantly in Arabia, India and the east coast of Africa. Queen Hatschepsut of Egypt sent an expedition to Somalia to bring back these precious trees for planting. Early harvests show the resin reddish in colour; aged and more precious products are white.

Frankincense is an ingredient in holy anointing oil and was used in the consecration of priestly functions. God Himself gave Moses instructions how to prepare and mix it; it was most holy to the Lord. (Exodus 30:34-35) Pure frankincense was also used to prepare the altar for the showbread (bread of the presence), most likely as a cleansing agent and a sweet aroma to the Lord. (2. Chronicles 2:4) As a gift to Christ it was symbolic of His divine priesthood.

The early Christian Church forbade the use of incense, considering it a heathen practise; this prohibition was changed by the emperor, Constantine in the 4th century.

GENEALOGY OF JESUS CHRIST

Matthew 1:1-17: *The book of the genealogy of Jesus Christ, the son of David, the son of Abraham. Abraham was the father of Isaac, and Isaac the father of Jacob, and Jacob the father of Judah and his brothers, and Judah the father of Perez and Zerah by Tamar, and Perez the father of Hezron, and Hezron the father of Ram, and Ram the father of Amminadab, and Amminadab the father of Nashon, and Nashon the father of Salmon, and Salmon the father of Boaz by Rahab, and Boaz the father of Obed by Ruth, and Obed the father of Jesse, and Jesse the father of David the king. And David was the father of Solomon by the wife of Uriah, and Solomon the father of Rehoboam, and Rehoboam the father of Abijah, and Abijah the father of Asa, and Asa the father of Jehoshaphat, and Jehoshaphat the father of Joram, and Joram the father of Uzziah, and Uzziah the father of Jotham, and Jotham the father of Ahaz, and Ahaz the father of Hezekiah, and Hezekiah the father of Manasseh, and Manasse the father of Amos, and Amos the father of Josiah, and Josiah the father of Jechoniah and his brothers, at the time of the deportation to Babylon.*

And after the deportation to Babylon: Jechoniah was the father of Shealtiel, and Shealtiel the father of Zerubbabel, and Zerubbabel the father of Abiud, and Abiud the father of Eliakim, and Eliakim the father of Azor, and Azor the father of Zadok, and Zadoc the father of Achim, and Achim the father of Eliud, and Eliud the father of Eleazor, and Eleazor the father of Mattan, and Mattan the father of Jacob, and Jacob the father of Joseph the husband of Mary, of whom Jesus was born, who is called Christ. So all the generations from Abraham to David were fourteen generations, and from David to the deportation to Babylon fourteen generations, and from the deportation to Babylon to the Christ fourteen generations.

Luke 3:23: *Jesus, when He began His ministry, was about thirty years of age, being the son (as was supposed) of Joseph, the son of Heli, the son of Matthat, the son of Levi, the son of Melchi, the son of Jannai, the son of Joseph, the son of Matthathias, the son of Jannai, the son of Amos, the son of Nahum, the son of Esli, the son of Naggai, the son of Maath, the son of Mattathias, the son of Semein, the son of Josech, the son of Joda, the son of Joanan, the son of Rhesa, the son of Zerubbabel, the son of Shealtiel, the son of Neri, the son of Melchi, the son of Addi, the son of Cosam, the son of Elmadam, the son of Er, the son of Joshua, the son of Eliezer, the son of Jorim, the son of Matthat, the son of Levi, the son of Simeon, the son of Judah, the son of Joseph, the son of Jonam, the son of Eliakim, the son of Meelea, the son of Menna, the son of Mattatah, the son of Nathan, the son of David, the son of Jesse, the son of Obed, the son of Boaz, the son of Sala, the son of Nashon, the son of Amminadab, the son of Admin, the son of Arni, the son of Hezron, the son of Perez, the son of Judah, the son of Jacob, the son of Isaac, the son of Abraham, the son of Terah, the son of Nahor, the son of Serug, the son of Reu, the son of Peleg, the son of Eber, the son of Shelah, the son of Cainan, the son of Arphaxad, the son of Shem, the son of Noah, the son of Lamech, the son of Methuselah, the son of Enoch, the son of Jared, the son of Mahalaleel, the son of Cainan, the son of Enos, the son of Seth, the son of Adam, the son of God.*

GIFTS

The notion of giving gifts at Christmas was a long time in coming since Christmas itself was not celebrated until later centuries. How it all started can probably never be exactly pinpointed, except to say that Christmas was God's gift to mankind: *For God so loved the world that he gave his only Son, that whoever believes in him should not perish but have eternal life. For God sent the Son into the world, not to condemn the world, but that the world might be saved through him. He who believes in him is not condemned; he who does not believe is condemned already, because he has not believed in the name of the only Son of God.* (John 3:16-18)

The next picture we have of gift-giving is of the Wise Men, bringing gold, frankincense and myrrh. The shepherds before them may have offered presents of fleeces and food, although we are not told. Since Christmas is the celebration of love, it was easy for the sentiment of love to express itself in tangible ways. It may have begun with useful things, and only later included superfluous presents. Most people in affluent countries would agree that this tradition has turned into a frenzy of shopping, charging, repaying and agonizing anxiety. Only by truly understanding Christmas and its reason and purpose can a proper balance be restored by individuals. It might help to always ask this question: does this gift reflect the Christmas spirit, does it reflect my love?

GLORY

The word "Glory" has a number of meanings, but it is always used in connection with God. When we think of the word "Glory", we think of light, splendour, radiance. God is light, and Jesus said of Himself that He *is* the light. John said: *In him was life, and the life was the light of men. The light shines in the darkness, and the darkness has not overcome it. The true light that enlightens every man was coming into the world.* (John 1:4-5, 9) In the Book of Revelation it says about the New Jerusalem: *And the city has no need of sun or moon to shine upon it, for the glory of God is its light, and its lamp is the lamb.* (Revelation 21:23)

In the Nativity story we read of the Angel of the Lord visiting the shepherds, who were watching their flocks by night, *and the glory of the Lord shone around them, and they were filled with fear.* (Luke 2:9) *And suddenly there was with the angel a multitude of the heavenly host praising God and saying, "Glory to God in the highest, and on earth peace among men with whom he is pleased!"* (Luke 2:13-14) Here the angels were literally "wearing" the glory of God; it was this glory that made them visible to the shepherds in the night. They also expressed "Glory to God"; it was a hymn of praise in words, perhaps in song. I have a sense that all of nature harmonized with the angels' "Glory to God"! Throughout scripture, whenever angels are encountered, the glory of God is seen, for angels are the messengers of the Lord, they stand in His presence day and night, and God's glory is transferred onto them, it clings to their garments like gold dust!

Since angels seem to have the appearance of human beings, the fear people experience when seeing an angel comes from the brightness of its being, as well as from the holiness surrounding it. The encounter of an angel means to be in the presence of God. And who would not tremble before Him! The Nativity stories give us a glimpse of divine and glorious encounters.

GOLD

One of the gifts of the Wise Men brought to the Christ Child was gold. Some of it may have come from Arabia, but it was also mined in other countries and was widely used for coinage and ornamentation because of its great value . Usually only royalty received such precious gifts, and the implication was that Christ was a King, and therefore deserved the best. Regardless of the shape or form this gift was in, it would have been a welcome mode of payment for lodgings and supplies along the way to Egypt.

GOSPELS

Gospel means "Good News" concerning Jesus Christ.

> The Nativity narrative according to Matthew: 1:18-2:23
>
> *Now the birth of Jesus Christ took place in this way. When his mother Mary had been betrothed to Joseph, before they came together she was found to be with child of the Holy Spirit; and her husband Joseph, being a just man and unwilling to put her to shame, resolved to divorce her quietly. But as he considered this, behold, an angel of the Lord appeared to him in a dream, saying, "Joseph, son of David, do not fear to take Mary your wife, for that which is conceived in her is of the Holy Spirit; she will bear a son, and you shall call his name Jesus, for he will save his people from their sins." All this took place to fulfil what the Lord had spoken by the prophet: "Behold, a virgin shall conceive and bear a son, and his name shall be called Emmanu-el" (which means, God with us). When Joseph woke from sleep, he did as the angel of the Lord commanded him; he took his wife, but knew her not until she had borne a son; and he called his name Jesus.*
>
> *Now when Jesus was born in Bethlehem of Judea in the days of Herod the king, behold, wise men from the East came to Jerusalem, saying, "Where is he who has been born king of the Jews? For we have seen his star in the East, and have come to worship him." When Herod the king heard this, he was troubled and all Jerusalem with him; and assembling all the chief priests and scribes of the people, he inquired of them where the Christ was to be born. They told him, "In Bethlehem of Judea; for so it is written by the prophet: 'And you, O Bethlehem, in the land of Judah, are by no means least among the rulers who will govern my people Israel.'" Then Herod summoned the wise men secretly and ascertained from them what time the star appeared, and he sent them to Bethlehem, saying, "Go and search diligently for the child, and when you have found him bring me word, that I too may come and worship him." When they had heard the king they went their way, and lo, the star which they had seen in the East went before them, till it came to rest over the place where the child was. When they saw the star, they rejoiced exceedingly with great joy, and going into the house they saw the child with Mary his mother, and they fell down and worshiped him. Then, opening their treasures, they offered him gifts, gold and frankincense and myrrh. And being warned in a dream not to return to Herod, they departed to their own country by another way.*
>
> *Now when they had departed, behold an angel of the Lord appeared to Joseph in a dream*

and said, "Rise, take the child and his mother, and flee to Egypt, and remain there till I tell you; for Herod is about to search for the child, to destroy him." And he rose and took the child and his mother by night and departed to Egypt, and remained there until the death of Herod. This was to fulfill what the Lord had spoken by the prophet, "Out of Egypt have I called my son." Then Herod, when he saw that he had been tricked by the wise men, was in a furious rage, and he sent and killed all the male children in Bethlehem and in all that region who were two years old or under, according to the time which he had ascertained from the wise men. Then was fulfilled what was spoken by the prophet Jeremiah, "A voice was heard in Ramah, wailing and loud lamentation, Rachel weeping for her children; she refused to be consoled, because they were no more." But when Herod died, behold, an angel of the Lord appeared in a dream to Joseph in Egypt, saying, "Rise, take the child and his mother, and go to the land of Israel, for those who sought the child's life are dead." And he rose and took the child and his mother, and went to the land of Israel. But when he heard that Archelaus reigned over Judea in place of his father Herod, he was afraid to go there, and being warned in a dream he withdrew to the district of Galilee. And he went and dwelt in a city called Nazareth, that what was spoken by the prophets might be fulfilled, "He shall be called a Nazarene."

The Nativity narrative according to Luke: 1:5-80; 2:1-40
In the days of Herod, king of Judea, there was a priest named Zechariah, of the division of Abija; and he had a wife of the daughters of Aaron, and her name was Elizabeth. And they were both righteous before God, walking in all the commandments and ordinances of the Lord blameless. But they had no child, because Elizabeth was barren, and both were advanced in years.
Now while he was serving as priest before God when his division was on duty, according to the custom of the priesthood, it fell to him by lot to enter the temple of the Lord and burn incense. And the whole multitude of the people were praying outside at the hour of incense. And there appeared to him an angel of the Lord standing on the right side of the altar of incense. And Zechariah was troubled when he saw him, and fear fell upon him. But the angel said to him, "Do not be afraid, Zechariah, for your prayer is heard, and your wife Elizabeth will bear you a son, and you shall call his name John. And you will have joy and gladness, and many will rejoice at his birth; for he will be great before the Lord, and he shall drink no wine nor strong drink, and he will be filled with the Holy Spirit, even from his mother's womb. And he will turn many of the sons of Israel to the Lord their God, and he will go before him in the spirit and power of Elijah, to turn the hearts of the fathers to the children, and the disobedient to the wisdom of the just, to make ready for the Lord a people prepared." And Zechariah said to the angel, "How shall I know this? For I am an old man, and my wife is advanced in years." And

the angel answered him, "I am Gabriel, who stand in the presence of God, and I was sent to speak to you, and to bring you the good news. And behold, you will be silent and unable to speak until the day that these things come to pass, because you did not believe my words, which will be fulfilled in their time." And the people were waiting for Zechariah, and they wondered at his delay in the temple; and when he came out, he could not speak to them, and they perceived that he had seen a vision in the temple; and he made signs to them and remained dumb. And when his time of service was ended, he went to his home. After these days his wife Elizabeth conceived, and for five months she hid herself, saying, "Thus the Lord has done to me in the days when he looked on me, to take away my reproach among men."

In the sixth month the angel Gabriel was sent from God to a city of Galilee named Nazareth, to a virgin betrothed to a man whose name was Joseph, of the house of David; and the virgin's name was Mary. And he came to her and said, "Hail, O favoured one, the Lord is with you!" But she was greatly troubled at the saying, and considered in her mind what sort of greeting this might be. And the angel said to her, "Do not be afraid, Mary, for you have found favour with God. And behold, you will conceive in your womb and bear a son, and you shall call his name Jesus. He will be great, and will be called the Son of the Most High; and the Lord will give to him the throne of his father David, and he will reign over the house of Jacob for ever; and of his kingdom there will be no end." And Mary said to the angel, "How can this be, since I have no husband?" And the angel said to her, "The Holy Spirit will come upon you, and the power of the Most High will overshadow you; therefore, the child to be born will be called holy, the Son of God. And behold, your kinswoman, Elizabeth in her old age has also conceived a son; and this is the sixth month with her who was called barren. For with God nothing will be impossible." And Mary said, "Behold, I am the handmaid of the Lord; let it be to me according to your word." And the angel departed from her.

In those days Mary arose and went with haste into the hill country, to a city of Judah, and she entered the house of Zechariah and greeted Elizabeth. And when Elizabeth heard the greeting of Mary, the babe leaped in her womb; and Elizabeth was filled with the Holy Spirit and she exclaimed with a loud cry, "Blessed are you among women, and blessed is the fruit of your womb! And why is this granted to me, that the mother of my Lord should come to me? For behold, when the voice of your greeting came to my ears, the babe in my womb leaped for joy. And blessed is she who believed that there would be a fulfillment of what was spoken to her from the Lord."

And Mary said, "My soul magnifies the Lord, and my spirit rejoices in God my Saviour, for he has regarded the low estate of his handmaiden. For behold, henceforth all generations will call me blessed; for he who is mighty has done great things for me, and holy is his name. And his mercy is on those who fear him from generation to generation.

He has shown strength with his arm, he has scattered the proud in the imagination of their hearts, he has put down the mighty from their thrones, and exalted those of low degree; he has filled the hungry with good things, and the rich he has sent empty away. He has helped his servant Israel in remembrance of his mercy, as he spoke to our fathers, to Abraham and to his posterity for ever." And Mary remained with her about three months, and returned to her home. Now the time came for Elizabeth to be delivered, and she gave birth to a son. And her neighbours and kinsfolk heard that the Lord had shown great mercy to her, and they rejoiced with her. And on the eighth day they came to circumcise the child; and they would have named him Zechariah after his father, but his mother said, "Not so; he shall be called John." And they said to her, "None of your kindred is called by this name." And they made signs to his father, inquiring what he would have him called. And he asked for a writing tablet, and wrote, "His name is John." And they all marvelled. And immediately his mouth was opened and his tongue loosed, and he spoke, blessing God. And fear came on all their neighbours. And all these things were talked about through all the hill country of Judea; and all who heard them laid them up in their hearts, saying, "What then will this child be?" For the hand of the Lord was with him. And his father Zechariah was filled with the Holy Spirit, and prophesied, saying, "Blessed be the Lord God of Israel, for he has visited and redeemed his people, and has raised up a horn of salvation for us in the house of his servant David, as he spoke by the mouth of his holy prophets from of old, that we should be saved from our enemies, and from the hand of all who hate us; to perform the mercy promised to our fathers, and to remember his holy covenant, the oath which he swore to our father Abraham, to grant us, that we, being delivered from the hand of our enemies, might serve him without fear, in holiness and righteousness before him all the days of our life. And you, child, will be called the prophet of the Most High; for you will go before the Lord to prepare his ways, to give knowledge of salvation to his people in the forgiveness of their sins, through the tender mercy of our God, when the day shall dawn upon us from on high to give light to those who sit in darkness and in the shadow of death, to guide our feet into the way of peace." And the child grew and became strong in spirit, and he was in the wilderness till the day of his manifestation to Israel.

In those days a decree went out from Caesar Augustus that all the world should be enrolled. This was the first enrolment, when Quirinius was governor of Syria. And all went to be enrolled, each to his own city. And Joseph also went up from Galilee, from the city of Nazareth, to Judea, to the city of David, which is called Bethlehem, because he was of the house and lineage of David, to be enrolled with Mary, his betrothed, who was with child. And while they were there, the time came for her to be delivered. And she gave birth to her first-born son and wrapped him in swaddling cloths, and laid him in a manger, because there was no place for them in the inn.

And in that region there were shepherds out in the field, keeping watch over their flock by night. And an angel of the Lord appeared to them, and the glory of the Lord shone around them, and they were filled with fear. And the angel said to them, "Be not afraid; for behold, I bring you good news of a great joy which will come to all the people; for to you is born this day in the city of David a Saviour, who is Christ the Lord. And this will be a sign for you: you will find a babe wrapped in swaddling cloths and lying in a manger." And suddenly there was with the angel a multitude of the heavenly host praising God and saying, "Glory to God in the highest, and on earth peace among men with whom he is pleased!" When the angel went away from them into heaven, the shepherds said to one another, "Let us go over to Bethlehem and see this thing that has happened, which the Lord has made known to us." And they went with haste, and found Mary and Joseph, and the babe lying in a manger. And when they saw it they made known the saying which had been told them concerning this child; and all who heard it wondered at what the shepherds told them. But Mary kept all these things, pondering them in her heart. And the shepherds returned, glorifying and praising God for all they had heard and seen, as it had been told them.

And at the end of eight days, when he was circumcised, he was called Jesus, the name given by the angel before he was conceived in the womb. And when the time came for their purification according to the law of Moses, they brought him up to Jerusalem to present him to the Lord (as it is written in the law of the Lord, "Every male that opens the womb shall be called holy to the Lord") and to offer a sacrifice according to what is said in the law of the Lord, "a pair of turtledoves, or two young pigeons." Now there was a man in Jerusalem, whose name was Simeon, and this man was righteous and devout, looking for the consolation of Israel, and the Holy Spirit was upon him. And it had been revealed to him by the Holy Spirit that he should not see death before he had seen the Lord's Christ. And inspired by the Spirit he came into the temple; and when the parents brought in the child Jesus, to do for him according to the custom of the law, he took him up in his arms and blessed God and said, "Lord, now lettest thou thy servant depart in peace, according to thy word; for mine eyes have seen thy salvation which thou hast prepared in the presence of all people, a light for revelation to the Gentiles, and for glory to thy people Israel." And his father and his mother marvelled at what was said about him; and Simeon blessed them and said to Mary his mother, "Behold, this child is set for the fall and rising of many in Israel, and for a sign that is spoken against (and a sword will pierce through your own soul also), that thoughts out of many hearts may be revealed."

And there was a prophetess, Anna, the daughter of Phanuel, of the tribe of Asher; she was of a great age, having lived with her husband seven years from her virginity, and as a widow till she was eighty-four. She did not depart from the temple, worshiping with

fasting and prayer night and day. And coming up at that very hour she gave thanks to God, and spoke of him to all who were looking for the redemption of Jerusalem.
And when they had performed everything, according to the law of the Lord, they returned to Galilee, to their own city, Nazareth. And the child grew and became strong, filled with wisdom; and the favour of the Lord was upon him.

The Nativity narrative according to John 1:1-18
In the beginning was the Word, and the Word was with God, and the Word was God. He was in the beginning with God; all things were made through him, and without him was not anything made that was made. In him was life, and the light was the life of men. The light shines in the darkness, and the darkness has not overcome it.
There was a man sent from God, whose name was John. He came for testimony, to bear witness to the light, that all might believe through him. He was not the light, but came to bear witness to the light. The true light that enlightens every man was coming into the world. He was in the world, and the world was made through him, yet the world knew him not. He came to his own home, and his own people received him not. But to all who received him, who believed in his name, he gave power to become children of God; who were born, not of blood nor of the will of the flesh nor of the will of man, but of God. And the Word became flesh and dwelt among us, full of grace and truth; we have beheld his glory, glory as of the only Son from the Father. (John bore witness to him, and cried, "This was he of whom I said, 'He who comes after me ranks before me, for he was before me.'" And from his fullness have we all received grace upon grace. For the law was given through Moses; grace and truth came through Jesus Christ. No one has ever seen God; the only Son, who is in the bosom of the Father, he has made him known.

GREETING CARDS

An old saying goes, "Necessity is the mother of invention!" This phrase may have proven to be true. In 1843 Sir Henry Cole in England, who every year sat down to write Christmas greetings to all his family members, friends and associates, was wondering, if there wasn't a better way to do this just as efficiently, not only because this was a tedious job, but also because this year he was running out of time. He shared his dilemma with a friend, John C. Horsley, suggesting a printed greeting that would convey the same message and good wishes. Horsley came up with a folding card; in the centre the family was portrayed in a comfortable setting, underneath this picture were the words: A merry Christmas and a Happy New Year to you. The side panels showed members of the family handing out gifts to beggars who had come to the door for alms. Sir Henry Cole loved it! All he had to do was sign each card, address the envelope and off it went. Surplus cards were successfully sold. It was an instant hit with all who received it and beyond, since word of this invention spread fast and wide.

Whether this was the first Christmas card, no one really knows, but it may well have been. Regardless, the fact that people were not as sedentary as they used to be, moving around not only within Europe, but even crossing the Oceans to other places, including the Americas, made correspondence necessary. From the Christmas greeting card it was only a small step to the invention of cards for all occasions; however, Christmas boosts its biggest sales, with Valentine's Day a close second. The variety is countless, from serious to semi-religious, to secular and funny. Unfortunately, despite the fact that Christmas is about Christ, the Son of God and His act of salvation, it gets harder every year to find this sentiment graphically displayed and in verse pronounced. It is a tragic sign of our times.

GUESTS

Christmas and Thanksgiving are probably the most celebrated holidays in the Christian world, when everybody wants to be home. Home with family and loved-ones, surrounded by familiar sounds, sights, smells and traditions. Most people grow up with good and joyful memories, and these often shape our expectations and celebrations. It is not only not unusual to have guests at this time, but should be encouraged: the university or college son or daughter to bring home a fellow student from a foreign land; a lonely relative or friend, recently separated or divorced; a family still new in the city, etc., etc. To show the hospitality that was denied to the Holy Family and this Divine Child is to show real Christian love; to embrace and welcome a stranger reflects the love God has for us.

HEROD

Literal translation in Greek: Offspring of a Hero (HERODES). The birth of Jesus took place during the reign of Herod the Great. He came to power in 37 B.C. and died in 4 B.C. Because of his alliance with Rome, he was proclaimed "King of Judea" and "King of the Jews". His rule was marked by great political, economic and architectural feats; he rebuilt the first temple, which Solomon had erected, and which was destroyed at the Babylonian invasion, was later rebuilt by Zerubbabel, but had fallen into disrepair by the time of Herod's reign. As much as his regime was marked by prosperity and a certain political security, it was also marred by internal fractions; many members of his own family (incl. wives and children) were gruesome and ruthlessly executed to ward off assassination attempts on his own life and struggles for his throne. He knew no pardon.

Reading the Gospel account of Matthew 2: When the Wise Men, erroneously believing that Christ, the new-born King, would be found at the residence of the king in Jerusalem, inquired about Him, Herod was naturally alarmed. Summoning the scribes to search the scriptures where this new King of the Jews was to be born, they told him, *"In Bethlehem of Judea; for so it is written by the prophet: 'And you, O Bethlehem, in the land of Judah, are by no means least among the rulers of Judah, for from you shall come a ruler who will govern my people Israel.'"* (Matth. 2:5-6) Herod passed this information on to the Wise Men and sent them to Bethlehem with the request to *"Go and search diligently for the child, and when you have found him bring me word, that I too may come and worship him."* (Matth. 2:8) But the Wise Men were warned in a dream not to return to Herod, but to take another way home, and Joseph was admonished in a dream by the angel of the Lord to *"take Mary and the babe and to flee to Egypt, and remain there till I tell you; for Herod is about to search for the child, to destroy him"* (Matth. 2:13). When Herod realized that the Wise Men had not obeyed his command to return and report on the new prospective ruler of Israel, he felt betrayed, and in a furious rage had all children two years old and younger in Bethlehem murdered. This may have been his last brutal act; he died shortly after, his legacy of 'Great' stained with blood rather than crowned with laurels.

HOLLY
Also called ILEX, is a shrub that can grow into a tree. It has thick, glossy, green leaves, prickly in nature, and bright red berries. It thrives in winter and is for that reason in high demand as Christmas decoration and in bouquets.

HOLY
The ordinary Hebrew word for "holy" is kadosh; it means separated, consecrated, set apart for the Lord or for the service to the Lord. Christmas is often called the "Holy Season" because it celebrates the birth of Jesus Christ, the Son of God. Joseph, Mary and the Christ Child are referred to as the "Holy Family", and Jerusalem is called the "Holy City".

IMMACULATE CONCEPTION
The Immaculate Conception refers to the Blessed Virgin Mary, not to Jesus. Pope Sixtus IV in 1476 approved the Feast of the Immaculate Conception; this feast was declared obligatory throughout Roman Catholic Christendom by Pope Clement XI in 1708. On the 8th of December 1854, Pope Pius IX gave definition to this term that "The Blessed Virgin Mary was conceived without sin", and since then this date has been observed by the Roman Catholic Church as a Holy Day, a Feast Day. Most Protestant churches lean towards the belief that the BVM (Blessed Virgin Mary) was conceived in original sin through the process of natural procreation, but was relieved of original sin sometime before her birth or

by the grace instilled through baptism. Baptism was practised before John by the Essenes, a sect at Qumran near Jerusalem. It was possible that Mary had been baptised.

INCARNATION

God in and as Christ, became flesh. The second member of the Holy Trinity became flesh, i.e. a human being (while maintaining His divine nature) on the day of incarnation when the angel Gabriel appeared to the Virgin Mary with the announcement that she had been chosen to bear the Son of God.

INN

Inns for wayfarers along the trade route between east and west were no elaborate affairs; they usually had an enclosed court with a well and stalls for animals and rooms for people. The latter were void of furniture, and often windowless. Guests brought their own mats and blankets or coats for sleeping and provided their own food, as well as fodder for the animals.

Bethlehem apparently had an inn, but due to the influx of people who had come for the census, Joseph and Mary found no room in it. Mary was very weary, and her time to be delivered had come. The couple was directed to an animal shelter for the night, which may have been a stable, but was more likely a grotto. Grottos are numerous in the land of Israel because of the rocky terrain.

INNOCENTS, HOLY

For most people the Christmas story is a wonderful, heart-warming account of a baby born in a far-away land, in poverty and seclusion, with a few animals as onlookers, a few angels in the sky and a few poor and simple-minded shepherds as company. It seems to get a bit more interesting when the Wise Men from the East appear with their elaborate gifts. But soon after this visit, Joseph is guided to take Mary and the infant on an urgent journey from Bethlehem to Egypt. Even the reason for this unexpected, pressing necessity is explained in only one sentence: *"Rise, take the child and his mother, and flee to Egypt, and remain there till I tell you; for Herod is about to search for the child, to destroy him."* (Matth. 2:13b) Most narratives, poems, songs and plays don't elaborate or even mention the horror that followed; it is too unbelievable, too gruesome, too indescribable, too traumatic for young hearts and old alike. It does not fit into the romantic cocoon that has been spun over 2,000 years since then. So this painful, tragic and dark blot in history is left out: *Then Herod, when he saw that he had been tricked by the Wise Men, was in a furious rage, and he sent and killed all the male children in Bethlehem and in all that region who were two years old and under, according to the time which he had ascertained from the Wise Men. Then was fulfilled what was spoken by the prophet Jeremiah, "A voice was heard in Rama, wailing and loud lamentation, Rachel weeping for her children; she refused to be consoled, because they were no more."* (Matth. 2:16-18)

The Wise Men were guided by a star from the beginning of their journey to the end, when they had found the newborn child and had offered their gifts and worshiped Him. Now that the use of the star was no longer needed, God spoke to them through an angel in a dream and warned them not to return to Herod on their way home, but to take another route. This gave the Holy Family time to escape the danger. When the king learned of the Wise Men's violation of his command, he was naturally enraged and gave the order that all male children in Bethlehem and surrounding area two years old and younger should be killed. No one can possibly imagine the carnage! History does not reveal how many children were massacred, although Eastern calendars quote 14,000. Considering that Bethlehem was not a large city, this number is unlikely. But no matter how many lost their lives, each child was precious to the parents, the family, the society, to God.

To understand the full extent of king Herod's fury and character, it may help to know that he was terrified of death and of losing his throne. It is well documented that he drowned his brother-in-law who was a high priest; he killed his uncle, aunt and mother-in-law, together with other members of the family; he murdered his own two sons and some three hundred officials whom he accused of treason. To know that another King had been born in his domain was unacceptable to him, so hundreds of innocent children had to die. Although they were unaware of the reason for their slaughter, the Christian Church recognized early on that they died for Christ, in His stead, and beginning in the third century their status was officially acknowledged. The 28th of December was chosen as commemoration of their martyrdom. In the fourth century in North Africa a Feast Day (Memorial) was declared by the Christian Church, and by the sixth century this was a universal observance. Many believers and churches in our time use this day to intercede for all the children who are in disadvantaged situations all over the world, and especially for those who have been and are being killed indiscriminately for personal gain. The Eastern Orthodox Church commemorates this day on the 29th of December.

ISAIAH

The reader may be surprised to see a reference to Isaiah included in this literary work. Who was Isaiah and why is he featured in this list of Christmas glossary? Isaiah is one of the major Old Testament prophets, whose work began in the year when king Uzziah died, in 740 B.C., which marked the last years of the kingdom of Judah and of Israel, before the destruction of Jerusalem and the captivity in Babylon. Isaiah has given numerous predictions about the coming Messiah, His birth, suffering, death and resurrection three-quarters of a millennium before the event! His writings cannot just be read at face value, but have double and triple meaning. The most pointed and revealing is probably God's word to

Isaiah in regards to the birth of the Messiah in chapter 9:6: *For to us a child is born, to us a son is given; and the government will be on his shoulder, and his name will be called "Wonderful Counselor, Mighty God, Everlasting Father, Prince of Peace."* Any and all references from the Gospels, whether of Isaiah or other prophets, are well worth reading and comparing.

ISRAEL

The name 'Israel' denotes first and foremost the people God chose for Himself; it is the Jewish Nation and its people. Abraham's descendent, Jacob (his grandson by Isaac), was renamed by God 'Israel' upon his return from a visit to his forefather's country, where he had met and married his uncles' two daughters, Leah and Rachel. After twenty years abroad, together with his families, livestock and much wealth, he returned home to his father. When he crossed the brook 'Jabbok', he entered the land of his brother Esau, whom he had antagonized by stealing his birthright, and he was terrified what Esau might do to him. But God gave him a promise that He would bless and greatly increase him; during the night at the ford a man wrestled with Jacob all night, injuring him, but he did not prevail. He asked to be let go, but Jacob answered, *"I will not let you go unless you bless me". And he said to him, "What is your name?" And he said, "Jacob". Then he said, "Your name shall no more be called Jacob, but Israel, for you have striven with God and with men, and have prevailed."* (Genesis 32:26-28) This was not merely a name-change, this was a historical and divine event. The injury Jacob sustained when God touched the sinew of his hip caused the Israelites from that day on to avoid eating the sinews (tendons) of the hind legs of any animal in respect of that event.

JERUSALEM

Also called 'Holy City', 'The City of God', 'The City of David'. The earliest Biblical reference comes from Genesis 14:18, where Melchizedek, king of Salem, as the city was then called, met and blessed Abram after the defeat of Ched-or-lao'mer by bringing him bread and wine. Jerusalem features prominently in the Nativity story because Bethlehem lies only 8 km south of the great city, and the Wise Men first went there to the palace of Herod to inquire about the new-born King which unleashed a whole avalanche of events: Joseph, warned in a dream, immediately packed up and fled with Mary and the infant Jesus, possibly along the trade route and hiding among the hustle and bustle of a caravan, or selecting a more quiet and obscure way into Egypt, until the danger was past. King Herod, in a fury because he felt betrayed by the Wise Men when they did not return to him to report where the child was, as he had asked them, routed his army and had all the children, two years and younger, in Bethlehem killed. Jesus, later on in life, spent considerable time in the city of Jerusalem and ultimately was crucified and died outside its walls.

JESUS

The name JESUS was given to both, Mary and Joseph; to Mary, the mother of our Lord, by the angel Gabriel, to Joseph in a dream. It is the equivalent of JESHUA in Hebrew and Aramaic. It means YAWEH IS SALVATION, YAWEH HAS SAVED. Jesus is also called the CHRIST, meaning MESSIAH, THE ANNOINTED ONE. Throughout His life, Jesus embodied that name; the ultimate test came at the time of His arrest, sentencing and crucifixion, but His validity was assured by His resurrection. Most of what we know about Him and His life is written in the four Gospels, Matthew, Mark, Luke and John. The Old Testament provides hundreds of descriptions of Him; most of the rest of the New Testament writings are based on His life, from His birth to His ascension into heaven and on His teachings.

Jesus is seen as the SECOND ADAM; through the first Adam sin came into the world, man was separated from God and expelled from the Garden of Eden. When God sent His Son into the world as a human child with a co-existent divine nature, through His death and resurrection Jesus Christ reconciled humanity with God the Father.

The last book of the New Testament, the Book of Revelation, was dictated by Christ Himself to John, His disciple, and reveals His coming again in glory. According to His word, He will reign on earth for 1000 years, when there will be peace on earth. After a short interval, which will bring calamity, He will create a new heaven and a new earth and establish His dominion for ever and ever.

Saint Paul, in his letter to the Philippians, gives a fine synopsis of why God sent His Son, Jesus, from heaven to earth:

"Have this mind among yourselves, which you have in Christ Jesus, who, though he was in the form of God, did not count equality with God, a thing to be grasped, but emptied himself, taking the form of a servant, being born in the likeness of men. And being found in human form he humbled himself and became obedient unto death, even death on a cross. Therefore God has highly exalted him and bestowed on him the name which is above every name, that at the name of Jesus every knee should bow, in heaven and on earth and under the earth, and every tongue confess that Jesus Christ is Lord, to the glory of God the Father." (Philippians 2:5-11)

JOHN – The Baptist

A contemporary of Christ. At the time when John the Baptist was born, this name was not overly popular, (it is mentioned in some of the writings of the Apocryphal Books) so when the time came for him to be circumcised and named, family and friends were surprised that both, the mother, Elizabeth, and the father, Zechariah, a priest, insisted that his name was John; it means 'Yaweh has been gracious'. And indeed, God was: Both, Zechariah and his wife who had been barren, were old when they received the joyful news through an angel that they would have a son (Luke 1:5-80). Because Elizabeth and Mary, the mother of Jesus, were cousins, John and Jesus would also be cousins. John was destined to prepare for Jesus' ministry: He preached repentance and baptized people for the forgiveness of sins, and Jesus Himself came to John to be baptized. Many a time John was suspected of being the Christ himself, but he refused any accolades and always pointed to Jesus: "He must increase, but I must decrease". (John 3:30) His story is intricately entwined with the Nativity of Christ that it cannot be separated without mutilating either.

JOHN – The Disciple

John, a disciple of Jesus and author of the Forth Gospel. After the popularity of John the Baptist, his preaching on the necessity of repentance and forgiveness of sins, his teaching on godly living and his baptising for regeneration, many people were deeply affected and resolved to name their sons 'John' after this fire-brand. One of the twelve disciples whom Jesus chose was called John; he was the younger brother of James; they were the sons of Zebedee, and both, at the call of Jesus, left their boats and their fishing nets to follow the Master. John seemed to have been the youngest of them all and was often found sitting or resting close to Jesus. Perhaps he saw a father-figure in Him or simply enjoyed His friendship. As close as he always was in life, he also was in death: it seems that he was the only one who stood under the cross of Christ with Mary, the mother, and a few other women, and then, at the command of Christ, took Mary to him into his house to care for her. John later wrote the Gospel, as well as three letters and the Book of Revelation while he was banned to the Island of Patmos, Greece.

John's Gospel does not fall into the same category as the other three (synoptic) Gospels; he does not give us the Nativity story the way we are used to by Matthew and Luke, rather he approaches the event from the beginning of time through a spiritual perspective, *"In the beginning was the Word (Logos), and the Word was with God, and the Word was God. He was in the beginning with God; all things were made through him, and without him was not anything made that was made."* (John 1:1-3)

The Gospel of John 1:1-18 should be read, and reread with great care to fully understand the divine event of the incarnation of God in Christ. While the historical data and descriptions of the other Gospels are equally valid and easier to understand, the first part of John's writings allow us a glimpse into the plan and the heart of God the Father as no other.

JOSEPH

The husband of Mary. Both Gospel writers, Matthew and Luke, make it clear that Joseph was of the house of David, and despite the fact that Jesus was his adoptive son, he was counted to be a descendant of David. It is possible that Joseph was a widower; he is called *"a just man"* (Matthew 1:19), and God chose him for a very unique role: To give protection to Mary, a virgin, validity to her pregnancy and to help raise Jesus. The last reference of him is at the time when Jesus was twelve years old, and the parents took Him to Jerusalem for His 'coming of age'. Joseph may have died soon after, for later references speak of Mary only.

Joseph was engaged to Mary at the time of the visitation by the angel Gabriel and her conception. His first and very human reaction to the news of her pregnancy was to quietly divorce her. If he had blamed her openly for infidelity, she would have been publicly stoned to death. God guided Joseph through the mazes of this relationship and the following events by an Angel of the Lord, who appeared in his dreams: That the pregnancy was legitimate through the Holy Spirit of God; not to be afraid to take Mary as his wife; to call the boy 'Jesus'; to flee with Mary and the child to Egypt in the face of Heord's threat to kill him; to call him back from Egypt, and finally, to redirect him to settle in Nazareth, rather than in Judea. Careful reading of scripture reveals the immense care and love God lavished on Joseph and his growing family, so that His plan would be executed within the law with precision and compassion. Joseph was not just a "just" man, he was the perfect man for the task. But then, do we expect anything less from God?

JOY

One of the most used words at Christmas is JOY. There are a number of definitions of joy, but they can all be summed up by this: Joy is a state of happiness or felicity. Joy is always an expression of an inner condition of the soul. Joy radiates happiness; joy is not dependant on outer circumstances. Many letters of people, who wrote from camps and prisons, even shortly before their executions (like Bonhoeffer) radiate this joy; they looked beyond death and saw heaven (like Stephen, Acts 7:54-60), and heaven was joy. On the night of Christ's birth, when the angels proclaimed to the shepherds, *"Glory to God in the highest, and on earth peace among men with whom he is pleased!"*, they were filled with joy, despite seeing Jesus lying in a crib in an animal shelter, Jesus, who was co-creator with the Father and one of the Godheads from the beginning. The angels received their joy from the Father that the long-standing prophecy of Genesis 3:15 was beginning to be fulfilled. That is the joy that frames every Christmas and infects millions of believers.

JUDAISM

Judaism encompasses the whole religious development and belief system in a transcendent God, and the experience of the Jewish people, spiritually, culturally and socially, and it is the foundation of the Christian faith. It can be compared to a tree: The roots, Judaism; the trunk, Christianity; the branches, the many different denominations.

KINGS

Only the Gospel of Matthew in the Nativity story relates the visit of the Wise Men (Magi or Astronomers), but does not call them 'kings'. This title was bestowed on them predominantly through secular literature; however, there may be more truth to their real identity than is assumed. For more information, see WISE MEN.

LEVI

Levi was one of the twelve sons of Jacob. This tribe was set apart and commissioned by God to execute priestly functions. Moses and Aaron (his brother) were of this tribe, and the latter was the first priest designated by God for this role. Jesus Christ is linked with this priesthood on his mother's side: His mother Mary was a cousin of Elizabeth, wife of Zechariah, a priest on duty at the temple in Jerusalem shortly before the conception of Jesus. Since marriages were arranged by the parents of a man and a woman, it is very likely that the parents of Zechariah and Elizabeth took great care to arrange their union, choosing a Levite bride for Zechariah. In the Eastern Orthodox tradition, candidates for the priesthood must be married before ordination; those who feel called to the Office of Bishop are not allowed to marry.

LIGHT

Christmas is called "The Festival of Light". That is undoubtedly true; no other holiday is adorned and lit up like it! There are a number of reasons for this: First, the light points to Christ, who came into the world to be its light, as John points out in his Gospel. Jesus called Himself, *"I am the light of the world; he who follows me will not walk in darkness, but will have the light of life".* (John 8:12b) *"I have come as light into the world, that whoever believes in me may not remain in darkness".* (John 12:46) And, *"As long as I am in the world, I am the light of the world".* (John 9:5) Second, the Advent and Christmas season is, for some parts of the world, especially the Northern hemisphere, the darkest time of the year. That's why people, even long before Christ was born, celebrated the winter solstice, when the sun turned again towards the earth: The days would get longer with more daylight and warmth, and in a few months the earth would robe itself again in colour and bring forth new life and fruit. To help introduce Christianity, old rituals were simply changed into new ones and carried into the new calendar, into the new reality of Christian teaching and understanding. Third, most people in the Western world, regardless of religion or cultural background, go along and celebrate Christmas; it is a welcome break in bleak winter days and an opportunity to get together with family and friends, to give gifts, to be and make merry. And as we all know: There is no season when people use and display more lights, whether it's candles or electric bulbs, than at Christmas.

LUKE

The Gospel writer, Luke, was by profession a physician (Col. 4:14), which explains his explicit and detailed description of the birth, life, death and resurrection of Jesus. He most likely knew the family well, and in later years he also travelled with the Apostle, Paul and ministered to him.

MAGI – See WISE MEN

MANGER

This was a trough or open box in a stable designed to hold feed or fodder for livestock. Stables were mostly only provided at inns for caravans and guests; locals would use stables or shelters only in inclement weather and for domestic animals like cows, goats, oxen and fowl. Sheep and non-milking goats would be out in pasture and hardly ever needed shelter, although temperatures can drop severely in that region in winter. Since existing stables were no more than caves or grottos – caverns in the natural stone formation of the land – it is very likely that mangers were likewise not made of wood, as we see depicted in pictures, but hewn out of stone. There are three reasons for this assumption: First, Palestine was not blessed with an abundance of forests, as a matter of fact, wood was scarce and had to be imported for construction (mostly from Lebanon) as we read in the Old Testament; it would have been much too expensive to be used for feed boxes for cattle. Second, cribs made from stone would have been easier to keep clean and last longer; animals invariably love to chew on wood, either they like the taste (since most wood is sweet) or to sharpen their teeth. A wooden manger would not last long. Third, a stone manger would foreshadow the resting place of Jesus' body at burial. At any rate, the crib was not a soft cradle for a newborn baby, but a simple affair, caked with fodder and mucus and lined, most likely, with straw and hay. Part of the blame that most people do not know or understand what Christmas means can be aimed at some artists who have given the world a distorted picture of this sober and sobering event; most artists used their imagination, their knowledge of animal feed troughs; hardly any of them had ever been to the Holy Land to see first-hand what the conditions were – and are, I might add. The birth of Christ is more and more concealed or romanticized; the truth is too stark, too unglamorous. It wouldn't sell! The world's ideas of Christmas stand in complete contrast to God's idea of Christmas: His gift of Christmas is free for the asking; the world's Christmas is often a deception of fake love – at a price.

MARK

Mark is one of the four Gospel writers. He does not give us an account of the Nativity, but his Gospel is considered to have been the first, and his information was probably used by others as a base for their stories.

MARY – MOTHER OF JESUS

In Hebrew, her name would be Miryam, like the sister of Moses. That makes it a very old and common name. She was related to Elizabeth, wife of Zechariah, a priest and the father of John the Baptist. According to Luke, Elizabeth was "of the daughters of Aaron" (Luke 1:5), the first priest in Israel and the older brother of Moses. Thus Mary being a cousin was likewise of a priestly tribe.

In the Nativity story, Mary is the mother of Jesus, and although she was only later on called the Mother of God, because Jesus is God, she was the Mother of God from the time of conception. She was betrothed to Joseph, a carpenter in Nazareth. A betrothal was a valid union, although couples did not live together for about one year until marriage. She was very likely a young teenager at the time of the angel's visitation. She was rightly perplexed at the announcement that she would become pregnant by the Holy Spirit, the Third Member of the Holy Trinity, assuming at first that it was an ordinary conception. She was puzzled because she and Joseph did not have an intimate relationship as yet. When the angel Gabriel told her, that her cousin, Elizabeth, was also pregnant in her advanced age, she very soon made the journey to go and see her, very likely to get confirmation of the news, and to make sure she was not deceived by another spirit-vision, for there was no precedent for this occurrence , except that she surely was aware that the Messiah was expected to be born of a virgin.

The Christian Church has always seen Mary as the Second Eve; by the first Eve came **the fall from grace** and the expulsion from paradise; the Second Eve **received the grace** from God to become the womb for Jesus, the Saviour of mankind. The first Eve **took** the fruit from the tree of good and evil against God's explicit order; symbolically the Second Eve **gave** the fruit of her womb to the tree of the cross, the tree of redemption. God saw fit to involve a woman in the act of salvation, despite a woman's act of rebellion against Him and His command. Women all over the world have (and still do) suffered the consequences of Eve's fall from grace, but God has already, for a long time, reconciled women with His heart. Christmas might be a good time to meditate on this!

While most of the Christian Church has a more general view of Mary, the Roman Catholic and Orthodox Churches have preserved a higher status of her; she is regarded as having received special graces of sinlessness at the time of *her* conception in order to be the perfect vehicle for the incarnation of God. It makes sense, not only that this is a firm belief, but that God would do this; after all, Jesus received His human nature from His Mother, and if she was plagued by sin just like anybody else, He could not have been the sinless man that He was, and He could not have been the Saviour, despite His divine nature. The Roman Catholic Church also teaches that Mary remained a virgin after (the birth of Jesus) as before, and that the marriage with Joseph was never consummated. This may be based on Isaiah 66:7-8a, God speaking to the prophet, *"Before she was in labour she gave birth, before her pain came upon her she was delivered of a son. Who has heard such a thing? Who has seen such a thing?"* This was, by the way, also Martin Luther's belief, the great reformer of the sixteenth century.

As mentioned at the beginning of this article on Mary, most Protestant Churches believe and teach that Mary had other children by her rightful husband, Joseph. This is based on the scripture passage of Matt. 13:54b-56, *"Where did this man get his wisdom, and these mighty works? Is not this the carpenter's son? Is not his mother called Mary? And are not his brothers James and Joseph and Simon and Judas? And are not all his sisters with us? Where then did this man get all this?"* The Gospel of Mark, 6:2b-3 offers identical information: *"Where did this man get all this? What is the wisdom given to him? What mighty works are wrought by his hands! Is not this the carpenter, the son of Mary and brother of James and Joses and Judas and Simon, and are not his sisters here with us?"* There are also some passages in the Gospel of John 7 that refer to His 'brothers'. However, all these may not have been blood relatives, but possibly children of Joseph by an earlier marriage, and therefore, stepbrothers and –sisters. Another explanation is that all these people mentioned as siblings may have been cousins. We know that Mary had a sister (John 19:25), and these may have been her children. The Hebrew word for brothers and cousins is one and the same. Nevertheless, what we believe about Mary, the Mother of Jesus, is not of consequence in regards to our faith in Christ and our salvation. But there can never be any doubt that she was, as the angel said, *"favoured by God"*, and in her Magnificat, her words were prophetic, *"For behold, henceforth all generations will call me blessed; for he who is mighty has done great things for me, and holy is his name."* This expression became part of the rosary. Mary is also called the 'Blessed Virgin Mary' (BMV).

From earliest times that artists have depicted the birth of Christ, the babe is always shown naked, while Mary, His Mother, kneels in front of Him, not in pain of exhaustion and woes, but in absolute adoration, exhilaration, joy, almost transfixed; Mary is in ecstasy before her Maker. The birth is described as having been as miraculous as the conception was. Religious artists have always been seen as people blessed with gifts of interpretation and inspiration; this is especially true of iconography in the Orthodox Church. Each icon is seen as a revelation from God. In the Nativity scene, the artists connected the nakedness, the total vulnerability of the child, with the nakedness and total vulnerability of Christ on the cross; to strip Him of His clothes was the ultimate show of repulsion for Christ who claimed to be the Son of God.

MARZIPAN

This delectable paste has nothing to do with Christmas, and yet, it is used at this time more than any other. One reason may be that almonds as well as many other nuts are harvested in the fall and are therefore readily available. So, please allow me a short culinary fling! After all, we are talking about Christmas and celebration and feastings, not fasting!

Genuine and pure marzipan consists of only three ingredients: very finely ground, blanched almonds, icing sugar and rose water (also called rose oil), the latter being available in most Drug- or Healthfood stores. Sometimes egg white is added to give it a more solid texture, especially if it is used to shape forms and to make tree decorations. The work is hard and tedious, and the right amount of each ingredient is very important, as well as the aging time. All this, however, is made easier through modern equipment and the availability of ready-made and affordable marzipan, often covered with chocolate, which is a nice combination.

The origin of this delicious confection is unclear. Persia and Arabia are mentioned in its history; it seems to have been introduced to Italy and other countries in Europe through traders and became very quickly a treat for the palates of the rich. Now, in the twenty-first century, pure marzipan is still expensive, but not out of reach for most people, and for many, like myself: the taste buds usually win out over concerns for expenses and tooth decay! So, enjoy!

MATTHEW

The Gospel writer, 'Matthew', was one of Christ's disciples. He was by trade a 'Tax Collector'; Jesus called him away from his accounting books to follow Him. Like Luke, he is meticulous in his report. That the Nativity narratives of these two differ somewhat should not be interpreted as conflicting, rather as additional information that may not have been available to each of them at the time of writing.

MEDITATION

Meditation is an exercise of the mind, pondering a thought or a passage, a book, a poem or a song, searching for meaning in one's own life or situation. It can be religious, spiritual or philosophical in nature, and often involves the heart and the emotions. Daily devotions of prayer and reading of the Bible is an act of meditation.

MESSIAH

The Hebrew word for 'Messiah' is MASHIAKH, the Anointed One, the Christ. He was expected to be a charismatic King of the Hebrews and their deliverer. Since the religious establishment did not know anything about Jesus' birth, they doubted that He could be the One. With His crucifixion and death, their suspicion was sealed, and He was dismissed as just another fake, since there had been many before Him. The Jews are still waiting for the "real" Messiah (in their opinion), and many believed in Jesus then and do so now; they are called "Messianic Jews".

MIDNIGHT MASS

This Holy Communion service is usually reserved only for the two great Feast Days: Christmas Eve and Easter Saturday. On Christmas Eve, candles are lit to signify the Light (Christ) coming into the world; on Holy Saturday, the lighted candles represent the resurrected Christ coming forth from the darkness of the tomb.

MISTLETOE

This is a European semi-parasitic green shrub with thick leaves, small yellowish flowers and waxy white berries. Long before Christmas it was used in northern countries in pagan rituals, signalling peace. In Britain, a mistletoe twig is often hung above a doorway during the Christmas season; any female, young or old (and in between) caught walking under it, may be kissed by any male of any age! It is meant more for 'eligible' people, but can be great fun for everybody. Because of the humorous element in this tradition, 'kissing under the mistletoe' has become a world-wide practise.

MUSIC

Is it imaginable to have Christmas without music? Without Handel's MESSIAH, JOY TO THE WORLD and all the other hundreds of carols we sing or listen to? Would we want to miss AWAY IN A MANGER, or THE LITTLE DRUMMER BOY, even the fun songs like JINGLE BELLS, or the romantic I'M DREAMING OF A WHITE CHRISTMAS? They all have their place in the repertoire of the joy we celebrate. Whether instrumental or vocal music or both combined, it is an expression of gratitude to God for what He has done for us. We are not told that the GLORIA by the angels was sung, but considering these words of the Lord to Job, *"Where were you when I laid the foundation of the earth? ....Who determined its measurements,....or who stretched the line upon it? On what were its bases sunk, or who laid its cornerstone, when the morning stars sang together, and all the sons of God shouted for joy?"* (Job 38:4-7), it is fairly certain that all heaven and earth and all the spheres were singing and making music at the time of the birth of Christ, their creator! I love Selma Lagerloeff's ending of the story, THE

HOLY NIGHT; she writes, "It doesn't depend on lights, or the sun and the moon, but what is needful is to have eyes to see the glory of God." Apart from Mary and Joseph, the shepherds in the field were the only people who heard and saw the Glory of God on the night of Jesus' birth.

In the busyness of our Christmas preparations, do we focus our eyes and tune our ears to see and hear? Can we occasionally turn off the radio, TV and other entertainment devices and listen to – silence? We might be surprised at what we hear!

MYRRH

Myrrh is produced from the balsamic wood and bark of odoriferous trees, like the commiphora abyssinica, and is a fragrant substance used in anointing oil and for perfumery. At that time it grew predominantly in east Africa and Arabia, but is now cultivated in other parts of the world too. By scratching or carving fissures into the bark, the tree "bleeds" this pungent resin. Used as an elixir, together with wine or water, it helped to deaden pain: *"And they offered him wine mingled with myrrh; but he did not take it."* (Mark 15:23) It was and still is used for the embalming of corpses. As John records, *"Nicodemus also, who had at first come to him by night, came bringing a mixture of myrrh and aloes, about a hundred pounds' weight. They took the body of Jesus, and bound it in linen cloths with the spices, as is the burial custom of the Jews."* (John 19:39-40) Myrrh, like the other two gifts from the Wise Men, was a prophetic indication of Christ's Royalty and destiny. Myrrh was brought to Him at His birth, myrrh was used at His death.

NAZARETH

Since the town of Nazareth in Galilee is not mentioned in either the Old Testament, the Apocryphal writings, nor in Josephus' accounts, it is believed to have been a very small village of insignificance or a later settlement. Why the families of Joseph and Mary established themselves there is not clear; it may have been part of God's mysterious, but wise plan to allow Jesus to grow up in relative safety, security and obscurity until the time of His ministry.

Nazareth is located about 142 km (88 miles) north of Jerusalem, and with an additional 8 km (5 miles) to Bethlehem, the trip Joseph and Mary undertook to obey the census was a heroic event. Since Mary was nine months pregnant and nearing her delivery and both of them undoubtedly knew the prophecy that the Messiah would be born in Bethlehem, it was not an option for her to stay home. They knew that this was indeed the long awaited and anticipated King of the Jews, the Messiah, the Son of God; the census was not Augustus' demand, it was God's will. After Joseph and Mary's journey to Bethlehem, where the birth of Jesus took place and their subsequent escape to Egypt, they returned to Nazareth where Jesus grew up and learned His foster father's (Joseph's) trade of carpentry. Matthew makes this remark, *And he, (Joseph) went and dwelt in a city called Nazareth, that what was spoken by the prophets might be fulfilled, "He shall be called a Nazarene."* (Matth. 2:23) The documentation for this particular passage has not been found in the Bible, but we know that there were other writings that did not make it into the canon, but were equally valid. The fulfillment speaks for itself. When Jesus began to assemble His discipleship, we read in John of the following conversation between Philip and Nathanael, *"We have found him of whom Moses in the law and also the prophets wrote, Jesus of Nazareth, the son of Joseph." Nathanael said to him, "Can anything good come out of Nazareth?"* (John 1:45b-46a) It obviously did!

NEW YEAR

In the western world, the old year ends on December 31st, and the new year begins on January 1st. For many people this is the end of the Christmas season, a new cycle begins. For those who follow the liturgical calendar, Christmas time extends until the 5th of January, and the New Year's celebrations are just a brief interruption or an opportunity to enrich the Christmas festivities.

NUTS

A Christmas season without nuts is almost unthinkable! It is probably the most versatile fruit of the time; it is harvested just a few months before (in the northern hemisphere anyway), it keeps well, it can be easily stored, it is a wonderful fruity, nutty and delicious ingredient in cooking and baking, and who does not like to sit by the open fire, crack nuts and then watch with delight as the shells blaze up and crackle in the flames? Nuts were also used, together with apples, as an early Christmas tree decoration; they would be wrapped in gold or silver foil or coloured paper or painted, with hangers glued on, and hung in the tree. As the season wore on, the tree would be stripped of its goodies, mostly by happy and hungry children!

ORNAMENTS

Early tree ornaments, as mentioned in the preceding article, were mostly apples, sometimes, when available and affordable, oranges and nuts, later on gingerbread men and cookies of all shapes or tastes were added, especially hearts and stars. Whether these decorations were used before adding candles probably depended on location, wealth and ingenuity. Coloured ribbons, balls of wool and yarn were attached, which could later on be used in sewing and knitting. Commercially made ornaments were soon added and enjoyed, as well as tinsel, which began to appear in the nineteenth century. Electricity in the western world provided a more consistent, safe and less expensive means of lighting the tree. All these customs were brought to other parts of the world by immigrants, including the Americas, where settlers added their own touch by making decorations from popped corn, strung up and wound around the tree's branches, from dried rosehip, red holly berries and other available, natural products. It was inexpensive and wholesome fun for the whole family. And it still is!

The variety of decorations offered in stores nowadays is eye-boggling, to say the least. Home-made ornaments, paper stars, etc. are to be preferred over ready-made products; they provide times of invaluable family togetherness and fun, and the simplicity of the end result is usually more reflective of the Christmas spirit of the plain and humble birth of Christ. Check out your library for books on ideas and crafts.

PEACE

The angels' proclamation to the shepherds was, *"Glory to God in the highest, and on earth peace among men with whom he is pleased".* (Luke 2:14) Other translations use the expression, "who enjoy his favour" (TJB), or "Peace on earth to those on whom his favour rests" (NAB), or "with whom he is pleased" (Gideon's International). The Hebrew word for peace is 'shalom', which has its beginnings in the Old Testament and denotes a state of complete harmony, i.e. safety, security, health and welfare, prosperity, contentment and the absence of conflict. It also means a peace relationship between God and man. In the New Testament, the word stands for inner strength and tranquility for the Christian believer; even in the midst of trials and tribulations, complete faith in God and in His grace and power through the death and resurrection of Jesus Christ results in perfect confidence, trust and joy. Absolute peace for the Christian will be at the Second Coming of Christ, the bodily resurrection and life eternal with God.

PLUM PUDDING

This is a rich, boiled or steamed pudding, more like a cake, consisting of fruits and spices, usually served with a sweet butter sauce, doused with rum, and the whole concoction ignited at the table. It is a famous Christmas dinner dessert in England, which increased in popularity through 'Mrs. Cratchit's plum pudding' in Charles Dickens' A CHRISTMAS CAROL.

POINSETTIA

The poinsettia is a showy plant with leafy clusters that turn a bright red in winter. Because of the abundance of colour, the actual flower is reduced to insignificance, consisting of a few, small, yellowish buds in the center. Originally native from Mexico to South America, it is now being grown in hot houses in North America and many other parts of the world in various colours. The poinsettia has easily won first place among Christmas plants and flowers, with the Christmas cactus a close second.

PRAYER

The word 'Prayer' comes from the Latin, 'Precarius', which means 'to pray' and can take different forms:

Adoration, thanksgiving, meditation, worship, confession and supplication, petition, intercession – in words or in song. Basically it is 'talking with God', which implies not only speaking, but also listening for God's reply. Very few people take the time to do that, showing surprise if anyone says, "I felt the Lord was saying to me....!" God created us; He is *our* Father. Jesus redeemed us; He is *our* Saviour. The Holy Spirit helps us; He is *our* companion, and the whole Trinity of God is **our** friend.

At the time of the Nativity, three great prayers were offered: The CANTICLE by Zechariah, the MAGNIFICAT by Mary and the NUNC DIMITIS by Simeon. All three have been incorporated into the Prayers of the Church. The adoration of the shepherds and of the Wise Men, and the words they spoke, were their prayers! Our prayer at Christmas could be worded like this – very simple:

> *"Thank you, Father, for sending us your Son, Jesus Christ, to be a light in our world, to teach us how to live and to save us from our sin. Lord Jesus, there was no room for you at the inn. I offer you my heart; be pleased to live in me, and fill me with your Holy Spirit, that I may live to your glory here on earth and with You for eternity in heaven. Amen."*

PROPHETS

Prophets are divinely inspired people whom God uses to proclaim a message to a nation (like Israel), the Church (Christians), or to individuals. This message can have one of two meanings, as someone has pointed out: Fore-telling or forth-telling. Fore-telling is a prediction of things to come; forth-telling is usually an assessment of current affairs and an exhortation, a warning, an admonition to change for the better. A case in point: Isaiah of the Old Testament was a "fore-telling" prophet; most of his messages deal with the coming Messiah, the coming of Christ, His life and death for the sins of the world. There were many others with similar predictions, relating to the same events. John the Baptist, however, the greatest prophet of the New Testament, was a "forth-telling" prophet; he called people to repentance from their sins and sinful lifestyles. John told everybody "off", from disciples to house wives, from soldiers to religious leaders. His God-given job was to prepare Israel spiritually for the Messiah who, as a contemporary of John, was already among them.

Prophecy is not limited to an "either" – "or" situation. A brief look at the prophet Jonah in the Old Testament reveals both intentions; he called the people of Niniveh to repentance. If not, God would destroy them and their city, They all heeded the call, including the king, and the city was spared. However, several hundreds of years later the people had fallen into the same sinful ways, and they and the city were annihilated. Former prophesies about Niniveh came to a complete fulfillment: The city would be laid to waste and swallowed up by the desert, and it was! (Nahum 1:3; Zephaniah 2:13-15) In 612 B.C. the Medes and Babylonians destroyed Niniveh, and a natural disaster helped the process; the Tigris River overflowed its banks and swept much away. Nature continued to do the rest, obliterating and covering the ruins so that they were not found until the middle of the nineteenth century, when French and English archaeologists found the ruins of that legendary place.

Prophecy not only played a role in foretelling the incarnation of God, but just prior to the Nativity itself, Zechariah, the father of John the Baptist, foretold the mission of his son, namely to prepare the way for the Messiah. And Elizabeth, his wife, said to Mary when she greeted her, *"Blessed are you among women, and blessed is the fruit of your womb! And why is this granted me, that the mother of my Lord should come to me?"* (Luke 1:42-43) How did Elizabeth know? She was inspired by the Holy Spirit and spoke prophetic words!

Prophecy is one of the gifts of the Holy Spirit; it cannot be acquired. If it is a profession, it is God-given. It is a gift, combined with a call from God for a particular person, time, place or situation. Saint Paul highlights prophecy as a very important spiritual, God-given ability, *"Make love your aim, and earnestly desire the spiritual gifts, especially that you may prophesy. For one who speaks in a tongue speaks not to men but to God; for no one understands him, but he utters mysteries in the Spirit. On the other hand, he who prophesies speaks to men for their up-building, and encouragement and consolation. He who speaks in a tongue edifies himself, but he who prophesies edifies the church. Now I want you all to speak in tongues, but even more to prophesy. He who prophesies is greater than he who speaks in tongues, unless someone interprets, so that the church may be edified."* (1. Corinthians 14:1-5)

PUNCH

This favourite beverage most likely had its origin in Hindustan, a region in northern India. Its root words are PAC, or PANCA in Sanskrit, related to the Greek PENTE; all words meaning "five". The drink consisted of wine or alcoholic liquor, citrus juice, spices, tea and water. It can be served hot or cold, and the alcoholic beverages can be replaced with non-alcoholic drinks. This is a welcome beverage at any party, but particularly at the festive season of Christmas and New Year, when get-togethers, visits, skating parties, sleigh rides and carolling still take place, especially where children are involved.

PURIFICATION (Candle Mass)

Under the Mosaic Law there was a purification rite necessary after childbirth for the mother. For the first seven days after the birth of a son, and fourteen days after the birth of a daughter the mother was unclean. Then followed the time of purification, during which she was not allowed to touch any hallowed item, nor go near the temple or a synagogue so as not to defile it. This period lasted 33 days for a son and 66 days for a daughter. When the time of purification had been properly observed, the family would pay a visit to the temple, bringing a one year old lamb, or for the less wealthy, two pigeons or two doves for a burnt offering and a dove for a sin offering. (Leviticus 12:8)

This was also the time of the presentation of the child Jesus in the temple when the babe was forty days old to give thanks to God. As an offering Joseph and Mary brought two turtle doves, the offering of the poor, and here they encountered the prophet Simeon and the prophetess Anna.

Mary's rite of purification and the Presentation of Christ is still commemorated today, better known as "Candle-Mass" by some denominations, on the second of February.

PYRAMIDS

No, I'm not talking about the magnificent pyramids of Egypt, but rather about a usually handcrafted Nativity scene, made from wood, that is cone-shaped and may have two or three platforms depicting the birth scene at Bethlehem. On the lower level may be displayed Mary and Joseph, with the Babe in the manger, the ox and the ass. On the second level, up in the mountains, may be flocks of sheep and their shepherds, looking up and shielding their eyes; on the third level the messenger angel and a choir of the heavenly host. Trees might be strategically placed around the scenes. At the very top is a fan which is propelled by heat emitted from candles attached at the bottom and lit. The number of candles depends on the size of the pyramid; they are usually white in keeping with the simplicity of the event. This is a great attraction for children; it invites telling them the story, but because of the live fire from the candles, great care has to be taken to keep this display safely out of reach and under constant supervision.

Christmas pyramids date back hundreds of years and have their origin in the Erzgebirge (Ore Mountains) of Germany, now part of Poland, where men during the long and often unproductive winter months would take to carving: useful items for the household or toys for the children. Much of this would be sold at markets to contribute to the always sparse income. Because of the rocky terrain, crops were poor, and so were people. By the way, the figure of the nutcracker also comes from this area. It became especially popular through Tschaikowski's NUTCRACKER BALLET.

A word of caution: The fan on the pyramid must be turning at all times when candles are lit, or the wood may become too hot and scorch or catch fire!

QUIRINIUS
Although Quirinius held important posts under two Roman emporers, Augustus and Tiberius, there have been debates whether the record in Luke 2:2 that he was governor of Syria at the time of the census and the birth of Christ is correct. Historians like Josephus and Tacitus have slightly different views. The fact that the precise date and year of the birth of Jesus Christ is unknown, complicates the time table and a precise historical record.

RIBBONS
Ribbons have become an essential item for packaging Christmas gifts. The favourite colour is red, but green is also very popular, as well as gold and silver. The **red** ribbon, however, is a symbol of salvation: When the two spies from Israel went into the city of Jericho, they lodged with Rahab, a prostitute, who lived in the wall of the city. When the king heard of this, he had her place searched for them, but Rahab had hidden them on the roof under stalks of flax. Later, after the gates of the city were closed, she let them down through the window after receiving assurance that, if she tied a red ribbon to her window at the time of the conquest of the city, she and her family would be spared. This promise was kept, and Rahab is listed in the genealogy of Jesus. (Joshua 2:18; 6:22-23; Matthew 1:5)

SANTA CLAUS
"Santa" means "Saint", and "Claus" is an abbreviation of Nicholas. Saint Nicholas was a bishop in Myra (Asia Minor) in the fourth century. Because of his good works in his district and his love for the poor, especially for children, he became a legendary figure. In the Middle Ages he was the Patron Saint of mariners. In the last few centuries his persona has developed into a fictional character that is highly promoted through songs, stories and movies, and is, of course, greatly loved by young and old. Santa Claus, also called "Saint

Nick", is the Patron Saint of children. Before the twentieth century he was robed in white vestments, chasuble, mitre and staff as bishops are and was usually portrayed holding three golden balls, representing the Trinity of God. The red outfit was a product of the last century. Stories abound how Saint Nicholas helped his people in times of hunger and need and children and young maidens in particular; libraries are a good source to access these.

SAVIOUR

The name JESUS means SAVIOUR; Jesus came down from heaven to save humanity from their sins (wrong-doings). He did not eliminate sin, but gave Himself as a sacrifice to pay the penalty for sin (just as there is a penalty for wrong-doing in our judicial system). Another word for Saviour is Redeemer: When Jesus died on the cross, His blood redeemed those who believed in Him – past, present and future.

SHEPHERDS

Shepherds figure very prominently in the Biblical narrative of the Nativity story; they were the first people to whom God presented the message of the birth of Jesus. First, an individual angel of the Lord appeared to them in the sky and brought them the good news, then a multitude of the heavenly host became visible to them, praising God with *"Glory to God in the highest, and on earth peace among men with whom he is pleased!"* As these heavenly messengers appeared, *the glory of the Lord shone around them, and they were filled with fear.* These men were weathered, stout and fearless; they were responsible for flocks of sheep and goats, numbering in the hundreds. The darkness of the night was always an opportune time for predatory animals to make their advance, so the shepherds had to be alert and on watch at all times. The owners of these flocks had entrusted them with their possessions, and the shepherds were liable for any loss. They had to be fairly knowledgeable in their trade in order to properly care for these animals since illness and disease, famines in the land, robbery and predatory attacks were not infrequent.

Shepherds were poor people; they might own a few animals themselves, but most were owned by folks in the city. That God would favour them, rather than the well-to-do and prominent, is so amazing; it shows what He is like and that He uses a different measuring stick then we do.

SIMEON

At the time of the Purification Rite in the temple at Jerusalem, about one month after the birth of Christ, the Holy Family presented Him to God. At this time there was a man in the city whose name was Simeon, and scripture says, that *he was righteous and devout, looking for the consolation of Israel, and the Holy Spirit was upon him.* And he blessed God and thanked Him for allowing him to see his Saviour, and turning to Mary he said,

"Behold this child is set for the fall and rising of many in Israel, and for a sign that is spoken against (and a sword will pierce through your own soul also)" (Luke 2:25-35) – a word which Mary surely remembered when she stood under the cross to see her Son crucified and die.

SNOW

In countries of the Northern Hemisphere, snow is a common occurrence in winter, and the first snow of the season is usually greeted with joy and anticipation, specially by children. It is a gift of nature: Fields and forests, meadows and gardens are covered with a white blanket of precipitation for protection from the icy blasts of winter. The melt and the run-off in the spring soak the ground for agricultural work, planting and growth. In countries and areas where snowfall is normally heavy, skiing, sledding and skating, the snow-mobile industry, as well as winter fests and carnivals are relying heavily on cold, snowy weather. And what greater joy is there for children if school is cancelled because of a raging blizzard?! Unfortunately, the same storm can create havoc for road conditions and drivers of any kind. And yet, and yet.... What is lovelier than to wake up one morning to a hushed world and a new layer of snow, to go for a walk in a winter wonderland? For those of us who grew up with snow, it just doesn't feel right not to have any of the white stuff at Christmas. Please, hold your snowballs! Since we cannot change the weather, I suggest we accept it good-naturedly as it presents itself, good or bad. The choice is ours to love or hate it, to enjoy it as a friend, or to shun it as an enemy. Most people who have learned to live with nature, its generosities and furies, have acquired a certain nonchalance that controls their lives and expresses itself in their attitudes. Peaceful attitudes! Every gift asks to be handled with the same care and love it is given; snow is God's gift for the earth, where it is necessary; let's receive it in the same spirit with thanksgiving. We will be blessed and happier for it.

SPICES

The spices most commonly used with Christmas baking are cinnamon, cloves, mace, ginger, lemon, nutmeg, rum aroma and vanilla. Most of these are oriental spices, but are now grown world-wide. Since vanilla is the most desired flavour, there is a brief description under that title.

STABLE

The word 'stable' produces images of a wooden structure which houses domestic animals. This is how most artists depicted the Nativity scene of Jesus' birth, but neither Gospel narrative uses the word 'stable', only that Christ was laid in a 'manger', because there was no room at the inn. Of course a manger would be located in a stable, but most animal shelters in those days, and even today, were in that area natural grottos, since trees for lumber were not plentiful in Israel – as mentioned before – and wood was too scarce and expensive to be used for building purposes, except for homes. It is, therefore, very likely that Jesus was born in a stone grotto and laid in a stone manger, fore-shadowing His burial on a stone ledge in a stone cave.

STAR

The star, which the Wise Men saw, has sparked thousands of debates for thousands of years, with a careful eye on the prophecy in the Old Testament, Numbers 24:17a-c, *"I see him, but not now; I behold him, but not nigh: a star shall come forth out of Jacob, and a sceptre shall rise out of Israel."* The mentioning of a star here serves a dual function: The prediction of the future Messiah of the Jewish people and of an astronomical sign. Whether this was a supernatural phenomenon, the conjunction of orbiting bodies, a comet, a meteor or a nova, it was a construction by God's hand in fulfillment of ancient prophesy and a miracle, as much as the Christ-event was miraculous. The star led the Wise Men to the new-born King, and it should not be overlooked that they fell down and worshipped Him and offered Him precious gifts, which indicated that they knew without a doubt who this infant was, and it also revealed the wealth of the donors. The latter very likely afforded the Holy Family their flight to Egypt and back home, and in addition were a sign of Christ's Kingship and an omen of His suffering and death. (See GOLD, FRANKINCENSE and MYRRH)

This was not just any star; this was a star of magnitude and significance. It would have been in the making for some time and have ignited the interest of astronomers far and wide. These were learned men, religious men, who not only knew the skies and how to interpret the movements of the heavenly bodies, but they also knew ancient prophesies. (See WISE MEN)

Kepler, at the beginning of the seventeenth century, studied the rare conjunction of Jupiter and Saturn when he noticed a brilliant star nearby; it was a nova. These are known to become very bright, then slowly burn out. This particular nova was observed for another whole year before disappearing. Kepler was extremely excited by this discovery, and he immediately began to study ancient books to see if a similar conjunction had happened at the time of Christ's birth. It had: In 7 B.C. In his opinion, it could have lasted as long as two years. In 1614 Kepler wrote, "The conjunction of Jupiter and Saturn was definitely a harbinger of the miraculous star of Bethlehem. But that unexpected star was not of the ordinary run of a nova. By a miracle, it moved in the lower layer of the atmosphere." Kepler was not alone with this belief; in the fifth century, St. John Chrysostom wrote, "God called the Magi by means of their customary pursuits and showed them a great and extraordinary star, so as to astonish them by the size and beauty of its appearance and the way it travelled. Think it not unworthy of God to have called the Magi by a star. He did so to raise them to better things. When he had brought them and guided them and set them before the manger, he no longer addressed them by a star but through an angel."

It is interesting that the Gospel of Luke does not mention the star or the visit of the Wise Men. Many Christmas stories feature the star in connection with the shepherds, but that is poetic licence; the shepherds went to Bethlehem to see the God-Child lying in a manger on account of the angel's message at the time of the birth. They may never have witnessed this phenomenal occurrence, or if they did, it held no significance for them; they had already seen the Messiah, they had spread the news, now they were back with their flocks. But for two thousand years the star has had its place in the Christmas story, in fact, in many stories, in carols and on Christmas trees and is a beloved emblem in the paraphernalia of the season.

ST. LUCIA

In many countries where Christmas was observed and celebrated, people devised new customs to honour the birth of Christ, and many of these have become traditions and inspirations to this day. One such usage that is very popular in Sweden is the observance of St. Lucia Day on the 13th of December.

Very early in the morning, while it is still dark outside, one of the daughters of the house makes her rounds from room to room. She is dressed in a long, flowing white gown with a red sash and wears a crown on her head that holds lighted candles. She wakens the sleeping family members and serves everyone coffee or an equivalent hot drink, together with St. Lucia buns which would have been baked the day before. While she is thus engaged, she sings a song in memory of the Saint or a Christmas carol. The white dress symbolizes the purity of St. Lucia, and her servitude resembles the piety of the Saint. The candles indicate two realities: The light of Christ has come, and St. Lucia, from antiquity was regarded as a light for the Church.

Who was St. Lucia? She was descended of a noble family of Syracuse in Sicily. She lost her father while quite young, but her mother, Eutychia, saw to it that she had a good education, and she was raised with great devotion to God and to Jesus Christ in particular. Unbeknownst to her mother, St. Lucia had decided at an early age to dedicate her life wholly to Christ and not to get married. When her mother became very ill, the daughter suggested to visit the tomb of St. Agatha in Catania, to whom many miracles were attributed. The pilgrimage, prayers and devotions were successful, and the mother, thankful for her daughter's interference told her that at her death all her wealth she would bequeath to her and encouraged her to marry the suitor who was already waiting in the wings. But St. Lucia would not hear of it, telling her mother of her decision and suggested instead to give her possessions to the poor, which she immediately began to do. Upon learning of this turn of events, the suitor appealed to Eutychia for a change of mind, but his efforts were in vain. He then turned to the governor Paschasius, complaining that Lucia was a Christian which was at that time contrary to the edicts of Deocletian and Maximian. The young woman was arrested and persuaded to sacrifice to idols and to obey the emperor, which she refused. After all tortures and trials failed, she was gravely injured with a sword, but managed to fall on her knees in prayer to God, sacrificing herself to Him. Her last words were for the young Christian Church, that soon all would be well and there would be peace. This event took place in 303/304 A.D. St. Lucia's faith and courage spread quickly throughout the growing Church, and her name was soon introduced into the Roman Canon.

As the Christian faith received its seal of approval by the emperor Constantine, it quickly spread all over Europe, even to the northern countries of Scandinavia, and the devotion to St. Lucia became a part of the preparation for Christmas. St. Ambrose, Bishop, wrote in his book **On Virginity**: 'You light up your grace of body with your splendour of soul'. It is easy to understand how this devotion developed into the tradition that is practised to this day and has even withstood the changes of the Reformation.

STOLLEN

Also called CHRIST-STOLLEN, this is a sweet, fruity loaf made with butter and beef tallow, raisins, currents (a raisin of Corinth, a small, seedless raisin grown chiefly in the Levant) and almonds, flour, sugar, spices and either baking powder or yeast. After rising (if baked with yeast), the dough is rolled out into a large, round shape, then one third is folded over, placed on a baking sheet, and after another rising is baked. While still warm, melted butter is poured over the loaf and generously covered with icing sugar.

The baking of stollen goes back to at least the 14th century, when a bishop of Naumburg, Germany, gave a special privilege to the bakers guild to produce this delicacy, but there is also the legend that a few centuries earlier a bread baker in Dresden had a few supplies left over from Christmas baking; he mixed them all together and was inspired to make a unique shape as if the loaf was an infant, wrapped in swaddling clothes. It was appropriately called CHRIST-STOLLEN. Genuine Dresden stollen is always made with yeast. Stollen is nowadays exported all over the world at Christmas time, but in many countries it is locally baked. It is a favourite delicacy to enjoy with a cup of coffee or tea during the Advent and Christmas season. In commercially produced goods preservatives are usually added, although this is not necessary if the stollen is either kept refrigerated or in a cool place. Generally, it doesn't last long enough to go bad; it's a delightful and nutritious sweet!

STORY-TELLING

If ever there is a time for story-telling, it is the Advent and Christmas period! There are hundreds and hundreds of stories to choose from that it can be difficult to make the right selection. A few questions may be in order to ask: For what audience, what age groups are these presentations meant? Great sensitivity must be applied to safeguard the Christian belief, as well as the tradition of the family; there can be conflicting messages. Many secular stories, written in the true spirit of Christmas, as well as personal experiences of a miraculous or compassionate nature are usually well received. The very best presentation is always the reading of one of the Gospels to set the tone for the hour of literary enjoyment and stimulation. Furthermore, the Gospel narratives set the boundaries for accuracy and truth. For as long as people do not know what Christmas is all about, they will have no benefit from it, no matter how much the cash registers jingle, the presents under the tree accumulate, how many parties they give or are invited to, how large the bonus was this year or how intoxicated or sober people were. Only the naked truth of a Babe born 2000 years ago in a stable in Bethlehem, lauded by angels, adored by shepherds, visited and worshipped by Wise Men from a distant land, proclaimed to be God's Son and the Saviour of the world for the forgiveness of sin, can give real, divine peace which every human heart craves, that same peace the angels proclaimed.

TEMPLE

In connection with the Gospel narratives of the Nativity, the reference is to the temple in Jerusalem. It was first erected by king Solomon, son of king David, who had wanted to build a permanent house for the Lord; he was instrumental in the collection of material and man power, but the building itself fell to his son who began the work shortly after ascending to the throne in 970 B.C. During the Babylonian invasion, the temple was ravished and ruined, but by order of Cyrus, king of Persia, a number of captives which Nebuchadnezzar had taken to Babylon, including Ezra and Nehemiah (to read these books in the O.T. is highly recommended), were dispatched by king Cyrus, together with the sacred vessels, monetary funds and a delegation of workers to rebuild the temple in Jerusalem. But again, it fell into disrepair, misuse during the Roman invasion and the Maccabeen revolt and finally into ruin. King Herod, the Great, trying to win the favour of the Jews in Judea rebuilt the temple according to its precise measurements and instructions, but added massive surroundings. At the time of Christ's birth and during His life, the temple was fully functional, but fell again victim to destruction in 70 A.D. and has never been rebuilt since then. But God has promised that it will be rebuilt at the right time.

THE JOYS OF CHRISTMAS

TINSEL

Tinsel is fine, thread-like strips of metal sheeting, usually in silver or gold, which is used to decorate Christmas trees. This ornament became popular in European countries in the 19th century. Before there was foil, it was made of lead strips, but is now made of much less harmful material. Over the last century it has gone, more or less, out of vogue, since more distinct and descriptive ornaments have replaced old-fashioned traditions.

TREE

The Christmas tree is, in general, probably the most prominent decorative item of the entire season, and its history is as colourful as its trimmings can be. Evergreen boughs were used immemorial, especially in winter in the absence of flowers to brighten up the interior of homes as a sign of life and as a reminder that spring would return.

In the Elsass city of Schlettstadt in France at the Humanist Library there is a ledger that documents the purchase of a Christmas tree in the year 1521. But who invented this tradition? Perhaps it was no invention at all, but rather a discovery.

Legend has it that Martin Luther, the great Reformer in the 16th century, was walking home through the forest one cold and starry night, when he noticed the coniferous trees full of snow and ice sparkling in the night light. He stopped to look at this wonder, then, deciding that it would delight his children at home, he cut down a small tree to take to his family. At home, the tree quickly lost its sparkle when the wintry frost on its twigs melted. Soon, small candles, rolled from bees wax and with a wick inside, were fastened with wire to the branches and lit. Wheather this actually happened on a Christmas day, before or after, is not known. We cannot even be sure that Luther was its founder; at and since that time he was credited for a lot of things and blamed for equally as many. It is perhaps unrealistic to think that it was Martin Luther; would he not have mentioned it somewhere in his writings, perhaps in his famous Table Talks, essays, compositions or sermons? He was also too much of a theologian to miss the connection to the tree in paradise that produced the fruit Eve plucked and ate and gave also to Adam to eat – against God's command – which ejected the first human beings from paradise, the presence of God, because of their disobedience and catapulted them into the hostile environment of earth. God's antidote? God became flesh (like us) through Jesus Christ. Christ in the manger, Christ on the tree of the cross! When we look at the image of the Baby Jesus in the manger, it makes us uncomfortable to think that He was **born** to **die** – for us! The sinless Son of God for sinful man. This is the greatest puzzle that has ever confronted humanity. But the Holy Word of God tells us, "Indeed, under the law almost everything is purified with blood, and without the shedding of blood there is no forgiveness of sin." (Hebrews 9:22)

This is the point: To look at a beautifully decorated Christmas tree reminds us that, if we are repentant, our sins are forgiven, and we are free to enjoy the grace and love of God. The evergreen gives us hope for immortality, eternal life with God.

There are preferences whether it should be a live tree or an artificial one; a live tree should always be first choice, because the evergreen has been used since time immemorial as a reminder of eternal life. Furthermore, an environmental consulting firm in Montreal has found that a natural Christmas tree has a smaller ecological footprint since it is a sustainable natural product. These trees are generally grown as crops on farms and harvested for exactly this purpose. According to the findings, an artificial tree would have to be reused for more than twenty years to be 'greener' than buying a fresh-cut tree annually. The calculations included greenhouse gas emissions, use of resources and human health impacts.

It is a wonderful experience, especially for families with children (and dogs!) to go out on a weekend during Advent to a tree farm to select a fitting specimen; the owners quite often provide horse-drawn wagon or sleigh rides, as well as hot chocolate, and the benefit of fresh air is inestimable.

By the way, do you know how to tell a fir from a spruce? Here's a small tip: The needles of a fir are flat and have two silver stripes on the underside. The needles of the spruce are round. In general, fir trees are preferred; they keep a lot longer and last well into the Feast of the Epiphany, the 6th of January. It is appropriate to keep the tree until then. This day usually is a final celebration of the season and has traditionally become a memorial to the arrival of the Wise Men in Bethlehem a long, long time ago, although this was not the initial meaning and purpose, but rather the arrival of Christ, the Messiah. This is also the Orthodox Christmas. In general, the church year begins a new season with Epiphany.

At the beginning of the tradition, candles were the only decoration, but the connection between the tree in the Garden of Eden and the tree to celebrate Christ's birth was not lost: Apples, polished to a shine, were hung in the tree. Not only did they last well, but their delicious aroma mingled with that of the fragrance of the coniferous tree, and this combined scent is heavenly! Also, it was an inexpensive and locally available item. Other decorations followed, but simplicity in decor should be preferred to over-trim, but that, of course, is a matter of taste and tradition.

What to do with a tree after the season? Most cities, towns and villages have a well organized plan for pickup or self-disposal in a designated area. A church in Michigan came up with its own solution: In the evening of the Feast of Epiphany members of the congregation are invited to bring their tree to a vast open space at the church, where the trees are burned in a log fire, while the people stand, watch and sing Christmas carols and read and listen to various stories. This is great fun for children and adults alike. Of course in our time, the question always is: Is this practise environmentally friendly? And safe? A licence is obligatory.

TRINITY

The Holy Trinity is the inseparable unit of Three Persons in One God. The relationship between Father, Son and Holy Spirit is considered "mysterious" in Christian tradition since it defies all rational analysis. Although artists and theologians have forever tried to depict and explain its mystery, it defies human understanding and can only be accepted by faith.

The word "Trinity" is not found in the Gospel narratives of the Nativity, yet it is the very fabric of the whole story and event, and although it is not mentioned in the entire Bible, it runs like a red ribbon through all of scripture. The Trinity, consisting of God the Father, God the Son and God the Holy Spirit, or in other words, God the Father, Jesus Christ the Son and the Holy Spirit is the essence of the Christian Creed. In Genesis 1 it says, *In the beginning God created the heavens and the earth. The earth was without form and void, and darkness was upon the face of the deep; and the Spirit of God was moving over the face of the waters.* (Genesis 1:1-2) *Then God said, "Let us make man in our image, after our likeness."* (Genesis 1:26a) Here we have in the very first chapter of the Bible an introduction of the Trinity of God.

After Adam and Eve fell from grace by eating of the forbidden fruit, God immediately devised a plan how to rescue humanity. He said to the serpent, *"Because you have done this, cursed are you above all cattle, and above all wild animals; upon your belly you shall go, and dust you shall eat all the days of your life. I will put enmity between you and the woman, and between your seed and her seed; he shall bruise your head and you shall bruise his heel."* (Genesis 3:14-15) This is the first prophetic word that we find in scripture. It is the foretelling of God the Father that He would send Jesus Christ, His Son, into the world to atone for the sins of mankind. Since a blood sacrifice was necessary for this atonement, Christ allowed Himself to be crucified on our behalf, although He was innocent. The author of the letter to the Hebrews writes in chapter 9:22: *Indeed under the law almost everything is purified with blood, and without the shedding of blood there is no forgiveness of sins.* In this connection it is not insignificant that after the fall, the first sin in the Garden of Eden when Adam and Eve discovered their nakedness, *the Lord God made for them garments of skins, and clothed them.* (Gen. 3:21) Here animal hides were used for coverings and blood was necessarily shed.

The rescue operation began with what we now call "Christmas"; God sent the angel Gabriel to Mary, a young virgin who lived in Nazareth, to tell her that she had been chosen to be the Mother of God. Upon her humble **fiat** (*And Mary said, "Behold, I am the handmaid of the Lord; let it be to me according to your word"* – Luke 1:38), the Holy Spirit came upon her and the power of the Most High overshadowed her. In this very event the Trinity of God acted separate, but unified, and at the same time bonded again with man.

For God so loved the world that he gave his only Son, that whoever believes in him should not perish but have eternal life. For God sent the Son into the world, not to condemn the world, but that the world might be saved through him. He who believes in him is not condemned; he who does not believe is condemned already, because he has not believed in the name of the only Son of God. (John 3:16-18)

Throughout the Old Testament the Holy Spirit, the Spirit of God, is mentioned, but we also get the occasional glimpse of Jesus (Saviour) Christ (Messiah) as already cited, although not spelled out by name. For example, in the Book of Job, one of the oldest books in the Old Testament, Job, whom God calls His *servant* which is in no way a derogatory term but a name, an expression of trust, declares to his friends: *"For I know that my Redeemer lives, and at last he will stand upon the earth; and after my skin has been thus destroyed, then from my flesh I shall see God, whom I shall see on my side, and my eyes shall behold, and not another".* (Job 19:25-27a) Thus Job spoke a prophetic word that would come true in the future.

TWELVE DAYS OF CHRISTMAS

The twelve days of Christmas are part of the Liturgical Roman Calendar; they begin with the 25th of December and end on the 5th of January, the day before Epiphany. Although Epiphany is by many people considered part of the Christmas observance because it celebrates the visit of the Magi/Wise Men from the East to pay homage to the new King, it begins the **Season of Epiphany**, which runs until Shrove Tuesday. The following day, Ash Wednesday, is the beginning of Lent. That Epiphany is the Christmas of the Orthodox Church has already been mentioned.

URGENCY/HASTE

The Advent and Christmas days are for most people a hectic and busy time. We want it to be the perfect celebration, smothering the real meaning, the real event in gifts and debts, in boxes and paper, in ribbons and stickers, in cooking and baking, shopping and cleaning, not to forget the many decorations, inside and out. There is hardly time to catch a breath for a quiet moment, for time out to meditate and contemplate the reason for the season. But anyone who has ever dared to sit down quietly to think or pray, perhaps to read a short inspiring story, or just to listen to some gentle, seasonal music, will gladly share the wisdom of such a peaceful experience.

When scripture tells us that the shepherds said to one another, *"Let us go over to Bethlehem and see this thing that has happened, which the Lord has made known to us."* And *they went with haste....*(Luke 2:15b-16a), their 'haste' was just the opposite of our haste, our restlessness; they were driven by the joyful message of the angel that their Saviour, for whom they had waited a long time, had finally arrived, their expectation was at last fulfilled. How could they not hurry; this was a message of life or death. The message is the same today, and for us too, it is a matter of life or death.

VANILLA
Vanilla is the most used spice in any baking, and no less so at Christmas. It easily blends with other spices, giving off a wonderful and gentle aroma. It is produced by extracting the inner pulpy part of the vanilla bean, which is the seed of a tropical American climbing orchid. The aroma is readily available in liquid form or in seasoned sugar in almost all grocery stores.

VESPER
This word relates to 'evening', thus church services on Christmas Eve are often called 'Vespers'. It may include Holy Communion, but this rite is usually held at midnight and called 'Midnight Mass'.

VESTMENTS
The vestments for the Advent season are blue, over a white alb for the priests and officiating clergy of most liturgical churches (some still wear purple), and hangings on the altar, lectern and pulpit are also blue to reflect the penitential season, yet different from Lent. The designs and colours are not just a fancy of the Church, but have a specific meaning to highlight special occasions. The colour of the vestments for the celebrations of Christmas is white. For more excellent reading on the subject, the book of THE STUDY OF LITURGY, CHAPTER VII, 6 is very helpful.

VIGIL
The meaning of this word is to 'watch' and is usually observed the night before a feast day. Although it can be privately kept on Christmas Eve, this is rather uncommon, whereas the Easter Vigil is frequently used.

VIRGIN
The prophet Isaiah foretold the birth of the Messiah, saying, *"Behold, a young woman shall conceive and bear a son, and shall call his name Immanuel"*. (Isaiah 7:14b) Several other translations, including the New International Version (NIV) and the New American Bible

(NAB), use the word 'virgin' to describe the Mother of Jesus: A young, unmarried and chaste woman, who has had no sexual relations with a man. Although Mary, also called the Blessed Virgin Mary, was 'betrothed', that is, 'engaged' to Joseph, which was in those days already legally binding, she had no intimate relationship with him, and thus was a fitting vessel for impregnation by God the Holy Spirit.

WHITE

White is the colour of purity and the liturgical colour of Christmas (and Easter). In the church, the blue linens, paraments and vestments of Advent are replaced by white, including the stoles of the priests and (usually) the robes of the choir members. White also signifies simplicity and humility, characteristics of the simple birth of Christ. In Europe, many Christmas trees in churches are decorated only with white lights and white paper stars (usually hand-made) to symbolize the purity, humility and poverty of Christ; the effect is absolutely stunning and thought-provoking! For Christmas in 1984 the Woman's Group of a Lutheran Church in Ontario, Canada, made hundreds of white paper stars in different sizes for the tree. Its only other decoration were small electric lights. On Christmas Eve the congregation was amazed and speechless at the beauty of the floor-to-ceiling tree in its indescribable splendour! After the service when most of the people had left, one woman was noticed still sitting in the pew. When asked, if she was 'alright', she explained that she had never seen such a beautiful Christmas tree; it was not just a feast for her eyes, but also an extremely meaningful and touching experience for her.

WISE MEN and MAGI

The Gospel of Matthew (2:1-12) gives the only account in the New Testament of the Wise Men's visit to Bethlehem. They came from the East, guided by a star and travelled first to Jerusalem, the seat of king Herod, expecting to find the new-born King there. Bethlehem is only about 8 km (5 mi) south of Jerusalem. Sometime before arriving in the big city they lost sight of the star, because this was not where Jesus was born. After learning that the Messiah would be born in Bethlehem in Judea, according to the prophet Micah (5:2), they turned south towards the given destination. As soon as they were on the right way again, they saw the star; it stood over the house where the infant was. This may have been about a month and a half after the birth, and the Holy Family had by this time moved into more hospitable quarters. Either the rush for the census was over and better accommodation was available or through the message which the shepherds spread around throughout the country, the extra-ordinary event was recognized and better living space was offered. According to Matthew's account, the *Wise Men went into the house, they saw the child with Mary, his mother, and they fell down and worshipped him. Then opening their treasures, they offered him gifts, gold and frankincense and myrrh.* (Matthew 2:11) Joseph, since he is not mentioned, may have been absent at this time, running errands, perhaps working, or buying supplies for the homeward journey. The Wise Men would have spent at least one night in Bethlehem, for they were *warned in a dream not to return to Herod, and they departed to their own country by another way.* (Matthew 2:12)

There are a number of myths surrounding the Wise Men, sometimes called Magi or Astronomers and more often "Kings". In legends, stories and plays they are often pictured as kings with royal robes and crowns on their heads. Who were these Wise Men? While Matthew may allude to Isaiah 60:6, *A multitude of camels shall cover you, the young camels of Midian and Ephah; all those from Sheba shall come. They shall bring gold and frankincense, and shall proclaim the praise of the Lord*, other interpretations quote Psalm 72:10b-11, *may the kings of Sheba and Seba bring gifts! May all kings fall down before him, all nations serve him!* The possibility that these men were kings cannot be entirely dismissed; even under Roman rule, far-away countries were often still governed by kings, like Judea. It is also possible that some of them in the caravan were Kings and others were Wise Men, namely their Astronomers, travelling together since this was a very uncommon and unusual event: The appearance of a special star to indicate the birth of a Great King. Since it was well known all over the Orient that Israel was awaiting a Messiah who would be King over Israel, this special phenomenon was greeted with great excitement. Who would have wanted to miss out on this experience?

The Wise Men were most likely members of the priestly tribe of the Medes of ancient Media in Persia and of the Zoroastrian religion, living throughout the Persian Empire. It was considered their office to accompany important delegations on their missions. The word **Magi** is not to be confused with magic since the prophet Zoroaster, who established the religion in the 6th century B.C., was strictly opposed to sorcery, witchcraft and evil. If they were from Persia, they may have travelled for a whole year to get to their destination, and the phenomenon of the star that guided them, would have lasted for that entire period. (See **Star**)

Connected with the question, whether the visitors were Wise Men or Kings, is the myth that there were three because of the three gifts. Neither the Gospel narrators nor other sources give a number. In reality, it probably was a caravan of many people; they seem to have come a great distance over vast stretches of desert for which servants and animals were absolutely necessary, in particular camels, to carry riders and supplies. Also, that one of the assumed three was a coloured man, is fiction. Scripture does not give any hint of this, nor of their names, Balthasar, Caspar and Melchior; this is simply poetry, albeit a lovely accent to the true story. It is believed that their remains are entombed in the Cathedral in Cologne, Germany. The relics were discovered in Persia, brought to Constantinople by St. Helena, the mother of the Emperor Constantine, transferred to Milan, Italy, in the 5th century A.D. and to Cologne in 1163.

The importance of this event cannot be overlooked. The Wise Men were undoubtedly intelligent and prosperous men, and God's summons to them was not only to provide the Holy Family with vital gifts to sustain them on their flight to Egypt, their time there and for the homeward journey, but it was also God's sign and invitation to the Gentiles to recognize this King as the Saviour for the whole world, for all of humanity, not just for Israel. It was God's fulfillment of His word that He spoke to Israel through the prophet Isaiah: *"I will give you as a light to the nations, that my salvation may reach to the end of the earth."* (Isaiah 49:6b) The two apostles, St. Paul and St. Barnabas point out this prophecy in their sermon at Antioch (Acts 13:46-48). The message that the Messiah would be born for the redemption of both, Jews and Gentiles was also spoken by the angel who addressed the shepherds, *"Be not afraid; for behold I bring you good news of a great joy which will come to all the people"*, and it was repeated by Simeon when he said, *"Mine eyes have seen thy salvation which thou hast prepared in the presence of all peoples, a light for revelation to the Gentiles and for glory to thy people Israel."* The Wise Men were the first representatives of the Gentiles.

WREATHS

Wreaths and garlands are popular decorations for the season. They are made from evergreen boughs, in particular of fir, hemlock, pine and spruce, sometimes even cedar branches or ilex (holly). Their year-round colour and fragrance are a reminder of God's faithfulness to His creation.

X-MAS

This is an abbreviation of **Christ-Mass**, origin unknown. X is the symbol for Christ from the Greek letter chi (X) and is the initial of Christ. A negative meaning is sometimes attached to this abbreviation: crossing Christ out of Christmas, when in fact the letter X is used to the affirmative, as in elections, for example.

YULE

Yule is an old English word for Christmas, the Feast of the Nativity of Jesus Christ. Yuletide describes the Christmas season.

YULE LOGS

Some traditions have it that on Christmas Eve a large log is put on the hearth as a foundation of the Christmas fire that would burn all night long as a warm welcome to the Christ-Child and to keep the home cozy for the next day's celebration. In our time, in many homes real fire places have been replaced by automatic heating systems, so creative and ingenious minds have come up with a substitute for the old Yule log: A rolled-up pastry filled with cream, fruits or nuts and likewise decorated on the outside, usually garnished with a sprig of holly with red berries for greater emphasis and attraction. It has become a great favourite with young and old alike. And although it may not warm the home, it will warm the heart!

ZION

The first mentioning in the Old Testament is recorded in 2. Samuel 5:7. Zion was a citadel in the center of Jerusalem, occupied by the Jebusites, when David, newly crowned king of Israel, attacked and conquered it despite negative predictions: *"You will not come in here, but the blind and the lame will ward you off."* However, David was successful; Jerusalem was named the city of David and has retained that name to this day. The name 'Zion' is also symbolic of the Nation of Israel and the homeland of the Jews.

Epilogue

It would be the greatest satisfaction for me to learn that the readers of this book thoroughly enjoyed it and that it gave them wonderful memories and a renewed sense of the celebration of the real meaning of Christmas. It is like finding a treasure again that was temporarily lost, but now is found and has become even more valuable than ever before. My sincerest prayer is that the book will be a blessing to you every time you take it into your hands and peruse its contents, that it may kindle or rekindle your faith in God, our loving, heavenly Father and in Jesus Christ, His dear Son, who came to earth as a child, to live and teach and ultimately die on a cross to pay for our transgressions. It is the most valuable gift God has to offer and for us to receive. When we open our hearts for this great gift of love, we will experience a new joy that will transform our lives, it will be a light in our darkest days and a comfort in our deepest trials, and we will realize that this gift of love does not have a credit line; it is free of charge and is always available. *For God so loved the world that He gave His only Son, that whoever believes in Him should not perish but have eternal life. For God sent the Son into the world not to condemn the world, but that the world might be saved through Him.* John 3:16.

Bibliography

CHATECHISM OF THE CATHOLIC CHURCH
Publications Service,
Canadian Conference of Catholic Bishops, Ottawa, 1994

DER ADVENTSKRANZ UND SEINE GESCHICHTE
Dietrich Sattler
Agentur des Rauhen Hauses, Hamburg, 1997

DICTIONARY OF CHRISTIAN THEOLOGY
Peter A. Angeles
Harper & Row, Publishers, San Francisco, 1985

EERDMANS' HANDBOOK TO THE WORLD'S RELIGIONS
Wm. B. Eerdmans Publishing Co., Grand Rapids, Michigan, 1982

FESTIVAL AND COMMEMORATIONS
Philip H. Pfatteicher
Augsburg Publishing House, Minneapolis, 1980

KRIPPE UND STERN
Gert Lindner
Guetersloher Verlagshaus, 1961

LUTHERAN BOOK OF WORSHIP, MINISTERS DESK EDITION
Augsburg Publishing House, Minneapolis and
Board of Publication, LCA, Philadelphia, 1978

MANUAL ON THE LITURGY – LUTHERAN BOOK OF WORSHIP
Philip H. Pfatteicher,
Augsburg Publishing House, Minneapolis, 1979
Carlos R. Messerli

THE CATHOLIC DIGEST CHRISTMAS BOOK
Father Kenneth Ryan
Carillon Books, St. Paul, Minnesota, 1977

THE COLLECTED WORKS OF BILLY GRAHAM - ANGELS
Billy Graham
Inspirational Press, New York, 1993

THE HOLY BIBLE, REVISED STANDARD VERSION
Thomas Nelson & Sons, New York, 1952

THE JERUSALEM BIBLE
Doubleday & Company, Inc., Garden City, New York, 1968

THE LION ENCYCLOPEDIA OF THE BIBLE
Reader's Digest Association, Inc.,
Lion Publishing, New Revised Edition, 1986

THE LITURGY OF THE HOURS – THE DIVINE OFFICE, ADVENT SEASON
Catholic Book Publishing Co., New York, 1975

THE NEW WESTMINSTER DICTIONARY OF THE BIBLE
Henry Snyder Gehman
The Westminster Press, Philadelphia, MCMLXX

THE STUDY OF LITURGY
C. Jones, G. Wainwright
Oxford University Press, 1978
E. Yarnold, SJ

VICTORIES OF THE MARTYRS
St. Alphonsus De Liguori
Redemptorist Fathers, Brooklyn

WEBSTER'S NEW COLLEGIATE DICTIONARY
G. & C. Merriam Company, Springfield, Massachusetts, 1975

WHO'S WHO IN THE BIBLE
The Reader's Digest Association, Inc.,
Pleasantville, New York, Montreal, 1994

About the Author

Gisela A. Riedel Nolte was born in 1936 in Pomerania, about 48 km west of Gdansk, where her parents operated a small farm; that area is now part of Poland. After WW II, in 1946, the family chose eviction for the sake of religious and political freedom. They were moved – by train – to West Germany, where they settled first near Cologne, and a year later to Mettmann, near Duesseldorf on the Rhine. At the age of 21, Gisela got married and immigrated with her husband to Toronto, Canada; they later lived in Pickering, Ontario. After her marriage failed in 1976, she worked for a couple of years to get her bearings, then in 1982 attended Wilfried Laurier University and Waterloo Lutheran Seminary in Waterloo, Ontario, earning a B.A. and an M.Div. After her retirement from active ministry she was involved in taking humanitarian aid to countries like Albania, Moldova and Romania. In 1992, Gisela was part of "Mission Volga", an evangelistic outreach to Russia that had its origin in St. Paul, Minnesota. During the height of the war in Serbia, she was part of a group of people from Ontario, Canada, on a pilgrimage to Bosnia/Hercigovina to "stand with the people and pray with the people". Perhaps her experience with WW II made her realize the importance of solidarity.

Gisela has two married sons and three grown (two married) grandchildren. Her first great-grandchild, a boy, was born at the end of June, 2013. She resides in Ontario, Canada.